Lapwing's Song
Octave of Life

Inspired by Rig Veda

DEV BHATTACHARYYA

DEDICATION

To the Lord

He who knows the Lord within
For him church-doors are always open

*

Mithoo, Dea, Sonne, Kamryn, Logan
Departed Sha and Kay

CONTENTS

ACKNOWLEDGMENTS

My salutations to Acharya Vyas circa 3000 BCE, Sayana c. 1400 CE, Prime Minister at the court of the King of Vijayanagar. My acknowledgments to Skanda, Madhava, Mudgal, C. Kunan Raja, H Wilson, Fredrick Max Mueller, Swami Vivekananda, Sri Aurobindo, A.C. Bose, Sri Kapali Sastry, S.K. Ramachandra Rao, R L Kashyap and R V Jahagirdar who pioneered the work on the Vedas. It is so easy to stand over their shoulders and seek beyond what they found.

There cannot be a true rendition of the Rig Veda, and "Lapwing's Song: Octave of Life" is no exception, but in all its imperfections, I hope it will nurture a great awakening.

FOREWORD

Lapwing's Song, rhymed verses in clear English is an insight into the world's most ancient oral tradition - Rig Veda. I concur with the author's hope this book will nurture a great awakening. The sages made Rig Veda with more than ten thousand metered verses in Sanskrit divided into ten books. It has more than 2000 verses addressed to the cosmic power, the Mystic Fire named Agni, without the use of any sustaining story in it. Skeptics in India who have no knowledge of Sanskrit or Indian culture simply declare that the verses are simply prayers in different forms for receiving utilities like cows. A reader of this book will see the irrelevance of such views.

Each verse of the Veda lends itself at least to two distinct approaches for understanding namely the 'ordinary meaning' which relies on senses and employs reason, the other labeled 'intuitive or psychological, which depends on inspiration and insight. The ordinary meaning may suggest a prayer for getting cows. Even with the ordinary meaning, the words set an interesting insight. For instance, moderns are obsessed with the use of the word "I", in questions such as, "Who am I?" Rig Veda shifts its attention to the plural "we" (nah pronoun in Sanskrit) which word appears at least in 1600 verses of Rig Veda. Note "nah" is different from "na" (indeclinable), not counted here. The prayers for happiness, peace or cows are made for all beings, not merely the author. The word "I" or its cognates such as "mine" occur in only about 80 verses in the whole Rig Veda. The word "gau" in Rig Veda has several meanings such as the animal "cow", knowledge, earth and others as stated in modern dictionaries.

When the Rig Veda author prays for the gift of "gau", he is praying for the gifts of cows and knowledge for all persons.

Earlier, Jean Le May has given a beautiful translation of about 1000 verses taken from all the ten books, devoted to several cosmic powers or devas. Our author Dev Bhattacharyya focuses on the verses mostly devoted to the deva, the Fire Agni and a few verses to the deva Vishnu. He chooses the verses only from the first four books. By skipping the thousands of verses to other cosmic powers such as Indra involving heavy symbolism, the book becomes accessible and enjoyable to many readers. However, the striking aspects of Rig Veda such as the questioning spirit (1.164.35) or the attitude towards skeptics such as Nema about Vedic devas (8.100.3) get missed out.

I did not find the famous Sukta (10.125) by the lady seer Ambrini on the creative power of speech. She is the main teacher of many Upanishads sages as mentioned in the list of teachers in Brihad Aranyaka Upanishad. The introductory essay of this book is very useful. I will add a few more details. The Rig Veda mentions that all the beings and the things in the whole universe is permeated by a nameless supreme power stated as 'That One' (*tat ekam* in Sanskrit). 'That One' is not a dictator. His helpers are the devas (or the gods), cosmic powers of Light and Strength whose aim lies in all-sided perfection of all beings on this earth and others.

Of course, among the hierarchy of devas, Agni has many powers of 'That One'. For instance, see the verses from the Mandala One, chapter one in this book with numbers (2.1.11) and others.

Similarly, the idea of rebirth is spoken in modern parlance as applicable to an individual, disregarding the life of an individual connected with hundreds of others. Rig Veda compares our life with multitude of other lives as a journey in a ship along with many others. When the time comes, an individual jumps off this boat and travels in a new boat with different persons, and different experiences. Thus, the ship is both a home and an aid to journey.

Some relevant verses in Rig Veda mentioning rebirth are, 1.140.12 (book 1, chapter 140, verse 12), also (6.21.2, 10.59.6, 10.18.5).

"O Agni, for chariot and for home, you give us a ship,
traveling with the eternal progress of motion,
that shall carry across the births and across the peace,
our strong spirits and our spirits of fullness"

RV (1.140.12)

Does rebirth implicate transmigration? Same soul goes through many different environments, each ship furnishing an environment of that birth. The soul creates for itself the different environments and felicities in each birth. The motion is eternal and progressive. The goal is to attain all around perfection.

However, the Universe is also made of negative or hostile powers which initiate malice among individuals and conflicts among nations. Many cultures acknowledge the presence of such negative powers. However, in the Rig Veda, the supreme power 'That One' pervades over all negative powers, since there is only ONE all-pervading power and nothing else.

Negative powers can surface in humans because some humans welcome such powers. The well-known six enemies, 'lust, anger (*krodha*), delusion (*moha*), greed (*lobha*), arrogance (*mada*) and jealousy (*matsara*) are symbolically revealed through animals and birds in Rig Veda such as the vulture (*grdhra*) associated with greed as in 7.104.22. Prominent among the negative, dark powers are Vala and Vritra. Vala hides all knowledge and prevents it's spread. Vritra attempts to stop the cosmic efforts of distribution of essential energies such as water from reaching anyone. However, the Supreme Power (*That One*) does not interfere in their activities of demons but uses them in unique ways to help the other creatures.

People ask me whether Rig Veda uses symbols and secrets. I offer the answer "yes". Words symbolizing secrecy such as *apichya, guha, guhyam, nihitam, ninyam,* occur in 140 verses. Verse (4.3.16) is dedicated to this topic. The Rig Veda poets were great observers of celestial movements. The scripture 3.53.8 states, "Sun arrives from heaven in one *muhurta* thrice daily to greet all places". *Muhurta* is 48 minutes; Sun completes 6 one-way journeys, each journey in 8 minutes close to current calculations of 8'15". As the author observes, this book could promote the planting of a sapling in preparation for a higher life. Dev Bhattacharya is the herald of the wisdom in the ancient book to us in the twenty-first century. It is not a coincidence that the English translations of the entire Rig Veda of all ten thousand verses made its debut through SAKSHI books in Bengaluru, India in the beginning of the twenty first century. SAKSHI sells every year about 30,000 books in 7 languages on the Vedas.

Jan 14, 2021

- R. L. Kashyap

Vedas are the pillars of Indian culture. Men with wisdom acknowledge it. Vedas are oriented to the well-being of the whole world. The philosophy and way of life expounded in the Vedas safeguard the good for mankind. Excellent education, harmonious and healthy social structure, ideal family tradition, political practices with true welfare, harmonious life patterns, equality of all mankind irrespective of any distinction are propounded in the Vedas. The body demands health, mind needs peace, soul yearns for solitude – all these are found in the crevices of the Vedas. In short, Veda is a supplement for all needs. It is an ocean encompassing the microcosm and macrocosm. But to attain such, one needs to dive deep and fathom its depths. True seekers find myriads of ways; and those who skip in haste and overlook, loose their way. Veda knowledge is more relevant today than the time when the sages revealed it.

Vedas do not endorse Sannyasa (a mendicant's life) for self-realization. Everyone can attain perfection in every walk of life. There need not and should not be a rift between material and spiritual life; instead, both can go hand-in-hand in harmony – the eternal call of the Vedas. Love should ooze from every heart. Let creativity bloom. Let comfort, plentitude and happiness of all mankind flourish thereof. The world needs the knowledge of the Veda. Sages have shown a clear path of ascendance and evolution of human. We need to be abreast it and pursue it. For that, we must propagate the knowledge of the Veda far and wide. Dev Bhattacharyya's present work is a great contribution in this regard. Songs nourish human beings. Birds' songs elevate the mood of human beings. The Vedic song emboldens and divinizes the human spirit. In the Vedic songs, Dev Bhattacharyya intends to elevate and tread the path of divinity.

This is a song celestial and Dev is a wonderful singer. The oldest songs of mankind are now made available in a wider known language by Dev Bhattacharyya. Poetry is so natural to him. Hence, the translation is magnificent. Filled with Vedic thought, he has successfully transformed his ecstasy into Lapwing's song. Songs are the precise way of expressing ecstasy.

Seers claim that the 'Path to the Gods is aglow' (1.1.4), because of Agni. To realize this, one has to become intimate with Agni. Inner yajna is the way. Yajna is an act of collaboration with the Gods. All the mantras presented here in this book helps us to embrace the mystic fire. The Rishis 'Seek easy access to the divine truth, as a father unto his son' (1.1.9).

Mantras are words of illumination. Outwardly a poetic verse. In a deeper level, it is an expression of the ecstasy enjoyed by the Rishis at the peak of their askesis. A Rishi is not only a person in contemplation, but also a person of action. Mantras are creative expression. And, Dev Bhattacharyya has selected and translated the mantras which take us to our core and assist our act from there. This process is 'octave of life'. The work helps the readers to elevate the vision and progress in the consciousness. Dev has put his best efforts to grasp and present the 'Five Suns of Poetry, Truth, Beauty, Delight, Life and the Spirit.'

Mystic fire (Agni) expedites the Yajna for the seeker. Agni distills the sap, the Delight of Existence, from the works of seeker and travels to heaven to offer it to the devas (gods). He gains an intimacy with the heaven. He returns to the seeker from the higher planes. On the way back he faces opposition from hostile forces. He succeeds in the fight.

Moving forward establishes the luminous power obtained from Heaven in his daughter, Usha, the Divine Dawn. It is an obliged Usha who manifests in the seeker. Agni is the psychological power, and he rules the human will-power. When we invoke Agni, he manifests in us, grows as seed sprouts, like a baby assuming a full-grown shape in the mother's womb. He acts as a messenger, a father, a pathfinder, teacher and leader, heading us to an arena of consciousness.

Translated mantra:

Light fills the men's lord to a brim
From heaven descends a clear vapor
Agni brings to light, full of spirit again
A young host, blameless neighbor

(1.71.8)

In this spectrum of life, man is at one end and the gods at the other end. Reaching from this end to the other is the spiritual journey. Lord Vishnu comes to our assistance. He apportions the seeker with his share of truth. Vishnu marches with three steps. When man clings to him, it is ensured, he will reach the heaven along with Vishnu. The idea remains hidden in the scripture 1.155.4. See here the magnanimous translation of Dev Bhattacharyya:

We laud his masculine power
Generous, guardian, safe with compassion
He marched, with three steps to the high tower
crossed earth's realms for life, for freedom.

With my studies and experience, I endorse the concluding words of Dev Bhattacharyya, "The Lapwing professes the Vedas as an instrument in seeing the eternal in everyday life." Veda-lovers will definitely enjoy the content of mantras and beauty of translation. Let this collection aid the reader's journey towards divinity. Also, I convey my thanks to Dev for presenting this work to the world of Vedas.

Sarve janah sukhino bhavantu

Makara Sankranti (Jan 14, 2021)

- R.V. Jahagirdar

INTRODUCTION

A puritanical, red-wattled lapwing fears nothing. A prodigal land stretches beneath his large wings tendering no threat. Feigning his best, though formidable; his left wing down and right leg up; soporific and fierce, he cries. Astounded at the loudness, he stops, still airborne. He resumes his cry. Is it for his mate? Unlikely. Cry of survival? No. Why the shrill cry? Why so humane, almost asking, "did I do it?" Camouflaged eggs, he and his mate own, strewn on the ground, with a promise of much-wanted rain in the parched land. Vast is the lapwing's expanse, the white streaked wing detaches the mind to look at the star speckled land dispassionately. Lying back on the arid sand, he, the lapwing supports the heavens, a vedic promise perched on its elegant wings. Thoughts become words; words blur into action in that starlit night. Early formulae of thought-provocation rapidly point to four stars in an obscure constellation; obscure and still the square of divinity, light, freedom and immortality.

Swathed is the quiet of the star-speckled canopy by a sudden, new visitor. A shooting star, ignited, to the point of extinction clambers the void between the twinkle of Orion's scabbard to the musings of the large freckled bear.

The lapwing looks away, his eyes no longer focused at the celestial marvel. 'The universe may have come from a union of its highest parents, the eager-supreme and his active-desire. Who knows?' The lapwing remembers to hold it steady. There was a time the universe was different. There will come a time it will again be different. Simple rules. Just as life owes to matter. From life, progresses mind. But, mind, a construct of higher power, buries itself into the folds of Avagunthana[1]. Unwrap it, the lapwing cannot; but then, who can? A new cloak of consciousness?

The did-you-do-it lapwing bird even today announces at the end of day and beginning of night, his phantom shriek, a quick pointer to a rapidly invading star spotted gown draping the land below. When philosophers over-intellectualize and create problems where none exist, I turn to the lapwing. In the clasp of his claws, he holds the answers. Any philosophy, worth its name, he has mastered. Those powerful beacons, namely his claws, liberate us from the banshees of the night.

"The Veda," Frederick Muller agrees to the lapwing in his notes "I feel convinced, will occupy scholars for centuries to come and will take and maintain forever its position as the most ancient of books in the library of mankind."

---

[1] Avagunthana (Sanskrit) means a veil

Then comes to the mind what Aurobindo wrote in his notes. "Man's highest aspiration – is discovering that perfection; a longing he has for freedom and mastery and relishing the untarnished truth and unmixed delight that comes with it. This is in flagrant contradiction with the present existence and ordinary experience. Well, how does a person achieve it?"

The dormant Lapwing stirs. From dormancy to activity is this defiant awakening. Under the stimulus of a fiery, sweet Soma, does he pen the forgotten parables? He waters down the earlier ideals to the present needs of society, which are at crossroads on how to affirm higher and deeper experiences.

I, a renewed Lapwing, pause to deliberate on the workings of Aurobindo. "We speak of the evolution of life in matter, the development of mind in matter; but evolution is a merely a word which states the phenomenon without explaining it. For there seems to be no reason why life should evolve from material elements, or mind out of living form, unless we accept the ancient aphorism that life is already involved in matter and mind in life because matter is a form of veiled life, life a form of veiled consciousness."

Life develops from matter, and mind from life.
- ⊗ Matter is a configuration of veiled Life
- ⊗ Life, a structure of veiled Mind
- ⊗ Mind, a veiled arrangement of a higher power, the Spirit
- ⊗ Man's highest aspiration would then only indicate the gradual unveiling of the spirit within
- ⊗ In preparation of a higher life on earth

Rig Veda, the original, spoken not written, is well structured. Spoken Rig Veda arranges verses in its own subtle way. Every verse, a Mantra carries a unique expression. These verses scaffold a metrical rhythm. The Vedic meter of Chaandas is the fixed, balanced system that can measure sound by 'Matra', a unit of rhythm. Dr Kashyap explains in his book Rishi-s, that the ancient people recognized the spirit of creation who framed every movement in the world through Chaandas, in certain fixed rhythms of the formative word. Ancient forefathers represented such cosmic tempos through poetic metres. A balanced harmony maintained by a system of subtle recurrences conveyed to them the concepts of immortality. Even today, space and its quietude suggest eternity. Dr Kashyap explains, this musical sound-image fills, stabilizes and deepens our thought impression, transporting the senses into something ineffable. Seven metrical themes recur in the Rig Veda scriptures. The Mantra develops within this metrical verse, some parts owed to the crux, some parts to the rhythm. Therefore, any translator, worth the name can either stay faithful to the syllabic rhythms or stay authentic to the essence or let his reason guess the verbal syntax and intonations of the verse. In "Lapwing's Song", I stay true to the three choices.

Also, several deities[2] assume distinct roles throughout the books. The question that comes to mind immediately, are they deities or metaphorical constructs? At this point it becomes evident there cannot be a simple translation of the Rig Veda. Books one through ten carry a thousand odd Mantra's interspersed between many chapters.

---

[2] Rig Veda Verses 1.164.23

Several Rishi-s author the chapters. A chapter may have many Mantras, dedicated to distinct deities using special metres, the authorship, however, does not change. It is quite evident that oral scriptures in Mandala one through ten, became prone to external influences through the ages, where other authors added their own baggage of scripts aimlessly. The author-poets set the stage for Agni in every book's beginning. Mid regions in the books speak on Indra, Ashvin, Marut and others. Vishnu appears in just three chapters. Scriptures in Satapata, in the third Brahmana speak of a similar vedic thought. The text states, 'Come to our sacrifice. There's water, there's cake for the deities in eleven pots intended for Agni all the way to Vishnu.' As Agni represents every other deity, therefore, the offering to Agni becomes available to all deities. Agni is the lower half, and Vishnu, the upper half of any sacrifice. Why the magic number 11? The reference lies in Rig Veda book ten, sukta seventy-two. Satapata suggests an offering to the eight Aditya sons from Agni to Vishnu. Rig Veda 1.164.23 suggests from Aditi came Daksha. Returned Aditi to Daksha. It is a beautiful rendition of the cyclical nature of life. Sun assumes birth in the day to die at night. Death as we understand today has a circadian rhythm.

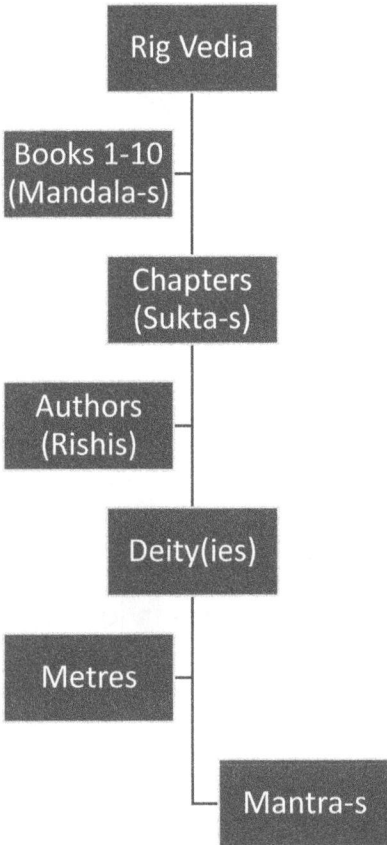

We proclaim generations of devas
In future, people will know them
Like a smith, Brahmanaspati blasts and smelts
Skilled he is in designing the devas
Smashes the truth from untruth[3]
Soon the regions[4] assume a shape
Earth springs from such productive power
And, Daksha is born to Aditi
But wasn't Aditi, Daksha's child?
After her, the blessed devas seek birth
Their friend in common is one, immortality[5]
Concealed in the waters, the devas clasp others in joy
Then, the dancers, their feet in motion
Rises a thick cloud of dust
Devas cup the universe like clouds
They summon Surya to the front
No longer can Surya hide in the sea
Eight sons of Aditi emerge into life
With seven of them, she goes to meet the heavens
But, she casts Martanda[6] away
With her seven sons, Aditi returns to an earlier yuga[7]
She leaves Martanda to live, to die again

---

[3] Brahmanaspati-reta sam kamri evadhmat. Devanam purvaye yuga-asat sadjayata. Authors have depicted Asat as non-existence. It is untruth, left to the readers to exercise their reasoning.

[4] Regions – dishayan.

[5] Amritabandhav – friends to amrita or what does not perish

[6] Martanda - Sun

[7] Yuga – Earlier Epoch or Era

Lapwing's Song maintains a similar structure to Rig Veda. Rig Veda is composed of ten books, where ten clans claim authorship - Kanva, Angira, Agastya, Gritsamada, Visvamitra, Atri, Vasistha, Kashyap, Bharata and Brighu. Lapwing's Song pauses at Rig Veda book four and adopts only Agni and Vishnu. The book references the original Rig Veda at the bottom of each sukta using the convention:

(book number)(dot)(sukta number)(dot)(mantra number).

On a quite different note, our cat lived with us for seventeen years. She was family. Her health was frail, right from the day she came to our world. Last June, she breathed her last. Her loss meant a lot to me. She was there for a reason, an intent best understood by powers above. Every squirrel, cardinal, crow, sparrow, ground hog that visits my backyard comes for a reason. I feel the reason; I cannot sense the logic. It defies logic, human logic operates only on terrestrial matters. Human speech, vocabulary and syntax are for human consumption, they fail to explain the divine. But every connection with a biped or four-footed creature owes its design to a higher purpose, a god send message only the heart can fathom. I suggest the reader look beyond the mere mantra-s into key cryptic symbols and metaphors that suggest the greater truth – that could promote the planting of a sapling in preparation of a higher life.

***

AGNI

With immutable Agni begins the Vedic journey, episodically culminating in the flame, collaborating with other gods. The illumined poet, several thousands of years before, lit a mystic fire in his falcon-like enclosure. Beckoned by urgency and his ardent devotion, the uncanny fire fueled the gods' quick summons requested by his creative rhymes. As his eyes strayed at the cluster of stars that smoothed a path to the distant north, he sensed the sky slowly turning bright – a bigger source of energy would soon be an answer to nature's summons. He could also sense; he was no longer alone. His long-gone predecessors and the spirit of the gods joined the microbial universe within him. Forgotten brothers-in-arms joined the mystic ritual. Merrily, the fire danced, the ancestral gods fanned the flames to a new day, a new beginning. He fathomed he no longer needed the fire. His insides were ablaze by a newfound revelation.

Agni in Rig Veda expedites a revelation, a series of unknown truths whose origin is not human. The ancient seers were the sole witness to the insights. They spoke of their experiences to their disciples, who recorded them verbatim. In the eyes of the seers, the fire came first, and the Vedas are replete with the divine dealings. A common pattern emerges on Agni, the metaphorical fire that expects to be the seekers friend, mentor and mediator. The supernal light to stay ablaze requires constant nurturing and control.

Outside the tenets of the ritual lore, only the seeker can nourish and fuel the flame. While the inner fire awaits constant kindling, it guarantees warmth and protection, and rewards the seeker with puissant light. The ratna-s or treasures become visible only in the fiery glow. With fire, an offering leads to a sacrifice, the unhesitating fire consumes the offering. The figurative inner fire scorches all I-ness and personal desires. Ownership is but transient – finally, the body along with things of delight turn into ashes. Reading the coded scriptures promotes different emotions; some readers treat it as a mystery, others - a treatise on economics. The Riks are not of human origin, but they are a divine enlightenment - an enlightenment that happens in the mind and completes at the heart. The interpretations often become difficult as one cannot comprehend an out of world experience and express through a written language.

> Veda is a rhetorical, recursive secret of itself.

Language of the Veda comes from the extraordinary flexibility of Mantra, an instrument of thought. Mantra can invoke in the prepared listener the same experience of that of the seer, the Rishi. It is like a voice within, within the head and heart that emotes the image of the untapped powers - a sabda roopa. A far cry from the degenerated rituals that the Vedas suffered all along in mediaeval times. The voice, its force and subtlety effects the individual and the ambience directly, where the Mantra remains to this day a creative living symbol. The ceremonial fire - Agni of Vedic worship symbolizes the sacred and supreme spirit. In the Rig-Veda, Agni is the "first born of creation," and is the pure and primordial energy of the universe. Rig-Veda tells us that this primal energy later transforms into several energies - of life Vaisvanara, of thought, Pragnya and radiation, Tejas.

In the Riks, the Vedic "word" labels as supreme, the best, unflawed crown of speech, concealed in a cocoon of secrecy from where it can manifest. There was a time when it was "visually heard" with no effort by the truth-seers, the Rishis, the powerful effects they could replicate on their track of speech; therefore, they diligently tutored their children and select disciples. The tradition continued and the code remained a treasured secret within a select few. On one hand was the power of the spoken word, on the other was its inner meaning. Those who cannot sense the inner code are like men who while looking, see not, or while listening, hear not. If you lend the mantras your ears or with a sharp knife of logic, peel the layers hoping to find a reason, you will discover there is no logic. Sri Aurobindo describes such a person to whom the Word is a tree without flowers or fruits. There is a key in the sacred hymns whose knowledge alone can throw open the truth and elevate a person to a higher existence.

While the universe cradles us, we in turn support trillions of inhabitants within. For those micro-organisms, that's their universe. They don't get a glimpse of the sun, moon and stars. Forces that drive the galactical world, moving celestial bodies are the same forces that pump our heart and steer our lives. Notwithstanding, they are the force that move the microbes within. We look with awe at the visible world, we imagine the black holes and nebulae; but barely think of the 60 odd trillion creatures inside us, never think of all the black-hole cavities within that make their universe. We are never alone (or is that a malapropism?). They are us; we are them; just like the supreme is in us and we are part of the supreme.

Every cosmic wonder is right there - within, then why the Euclidean and Einsteinian math to prove what is not us - we do not need a proof that we are. But we are (I don't quite agree with the "I am" notion) – and that's science, that's philosophy. Sixty trillion enjoy our life, our body, our wellbeing, and suffer the consequences of the death of our universe – how profound is that? But we never created that inner universe, it came free.

Madhucchandas

Agni ignites
The order of truth, he will herald
Sacrificial lord, the bejeweled ecstasies
Come to life in the glow once periled

1.1.1

Fire, bring with you every god
The ancient seers once befriended you
Sages of the new stay awed
Now, they adore you

1.1.2

They move to light's display
Many treasures arise from flame
Becoming more visible day upon day
Glory be your valor and name

1.1.3

Agni, a pilgrim of the Yajna[8] flow
Surrounds the flame
Path to the gods is aglow
The seers claim

1.1.4

---

[8]The closest definition of a Yajna is an act of sacrifice, an act of giving to the deities

The flame we strive
Summon the will of the seer
Hymns of truth - may they arrive
With the gods in no fear

1.1.5

A favored success is due
For the giver, Agni, you bring forth
Angira, truth alone is with you
Only you unearth

1.1.6

Mighty Agni's spot
Present by day, by night
We seek your grace by our thought
As we approach you in that light

1.1.7

To the monarch, bowed
Ruling the vast swathe
All is progress in his abode
He knows the shining path

1.1.8

We seek easy access to the divine truth
As a father unto his son
Nay, a state of happy and smooth
Where borders, there are none

1.1.9

Kanva

Agni, elected you are
The only minister who can summon
All knowing messenger, you are
The will in effect, sacrifice you've begun

1.12.1

Lord of creatures, accept my prayer
Adorations in plenty never dwarfed
To every flame, dear sacrifice achiever
My hymns to summon many a god

1.12.2

Agni, born you were here as in a dream
The gods you support swung by after
Spread is the chanter's seat, let the sacrifice begin
You are the Truth, summoning pastor

1.12.3

They wish to offer, awaken the author
And, when you tour, be our herald
Take a seat with the gods in honor
On this amazing holy grassland

1.12.4

Agni, offerings of charity call upon you
Your brilliance, let it oppose
Burn the radical haters before they brew
They who dare constrain with force

1.12.5

By the fire, impeccably kindled is fire
The seer, the house's young lord
This gift for you to admire
Consume it, O flame, keep it charred

1.12.6

Divine Agni, truth fills the law of being
Glow you will. Rescind all evil
My hymns of praise to the all-seeing
My approach, my chants prevail

1.12.7

O Agni, divine emissary
Lord of every offering, every tense
He waits on you unwary
Become a knight, become the defense

1.12.8

He comes with offering
Approaches your countenance, so divine
He launched the gods pondering
Distilled flame, your grace let it shine

1.12.9

Agni, glittering flame
Untainted in the land of paradise
Let the gods know of your fame
All our submissions and sacrifice

1.12.10

Adored, by Gayatri rhythms of chant
Bring to us, the contentment
O flame, by a hero's grant
Held you are in potent

1.12.11

Agni, glisten in the pure of white
Let the many divine hymns in concert
Hymns that summon the gods to a flight
Come and admit the hymn we assert

1.12.12

Fire, kindled you are with no flaw
Transport the gods to him
His offerings never withdraw
Agni, distill the sacrifice to gods within

1.13.1

Born of this body, set this sacrifice in flame
Make it honeyed to the gods
Spread the sweet syrup among them
O seer, they appreciate the odds

1.13.2

Flame, you they fancy
Hear my call. To this sacrifice, please come
Flame, you enact the offer when happy
Your honeyed dialect sets the norm

1.13.3

Fire, adored is your adept
Bring us the gods in your cheeriest car
What a man can only accept
None, you can send for

1.13.4

Stretched on a hallowed mat
Sages stay true to endurance and order
Speckled with a fuel of fat
All point to an immortal frontier

1.13.5

With all the deities, fire
Your action by words, we savor
You emerge before us set in the higher
Begin your labor

1.14.1

Agni, Kanwa calls on you now
You fire, are the wisdom's master
Eloquent turns the knowhow
Agni, appear with the gods faster

1.14.2

Indra, Vayu, Brihaspati, Mitra, Agni, Pushan, Bhaga all
Aditya and *Marut* - every god of might
Filled are nectar streams in rapture for all
Dripping sweet, much to everyone's delight

1.14.3-1.14.4

You, they adore, they favor Kanwa for you
How they manifest the flame!
How they make the offerings in new!
Their assortments, they proclaim

1.14.5

With fuel to the fire
The carriers harnessed to the mind
These cars carry the flame far
Bring gods to sip the Soma-wine

1.14.6

Adorable Agni, I greet
The truth will strengthen
Let their tongues savor the sweet
The wives and children

1.14.7

So adorable! At any sacrifice his preach
Agni, with your tongue, let them sip
Let them sip the fiery speech
To the rhythm of a sweet Soma drip

1.14.8

Flame, your world, the radiant sun
In the bright sky, poignant, resting upon
The seer, the offering's begun
Bring us gods who incite the dawn

1.14.9

O Agni, together
Let us relish the sweet Soma wine
Indra and Vayu pair
And lustrous Mitra are sure to dine

1.14.10

Agni, thinker and friend, so apt
At the hour of oblation, priest you are
Seated at the sacrifice, resort to act
Donation to the sacrifice we offer

1.14.11

Deity with reins, seated in a car
Crimson, rosy and green
Bring the gods from far
With colors in between

1.14.12

Wear your finest attire
Finest, O adorable fire
Mighty chief, purifier
Join our offerings choir

1.26.1

Agni seated young, strong
In supremacy, this sacrifice, you conduct
Meditative thoughts, you transform
Into a speech construct

1.26.2

He handles the sacrifice in wonder
As a father to his son
A lover for his love, a comrade to another
Such offerings are second to none

1.26.3

Varuna, Mitra and Aryaman three
Demolishers of every foe
Your sacred seat from a devotee
As human friends you bestow

1.26.4

An ancient priest's script
At the seat of the offering
Rejoice in our friendship
And these words to you, I bring

1.26.5

Durable possessions accrue
Complete the sacrifice to god
And, lord, it is always you
To whom, this offering we've sought

1.26.6

Our leader in this sacrifice dear
Supreme offering, he makes, in delight
We seek your grace Agni with no fear
Give us your strength and your might

1.26.7

Gained by the gods, a firepower
Holds firm, the supreme good
Bequeathed, our meditation this hour
Agni's strengths in burning the wood

1.26.8

A give-and-take plan
Full expressions of being and non-being
Immortals award bounties to mortal man
To the deathless gods in man's asking

1.26.9

Agni, enrich the strength you know
Approve the mastery with force
Force, my sacrifice will escrow
Force, my speech, this delightful dose

1.26.10

Blessed by swift showering strength
With an obeisance, let me adore you
The strong, fire king at length
How you rule the subjects below

1.27.1

Seeking your kindness, smothered in love
Your mood - happy, satisfied
Move you must, flashes of brilliance above
Reach many places, far and wide

1.27.2

Far and near spreads your safeguard
You constantly build that protection
Vibrant strength of the deities blows hard
Combat every ill health and infection

1.27.3

Articulate on the perfect
Here's a new chant we got
Fire, among gods select
It is a new powerful thought

1.27.4

Sunder not, we are stable
The mid-point, when we reach
Instill in us, make us able
O fire, please teach

1.27.5

Ornate and brilliant you sail
Swelling waters of the ocean past the reefer
The waters, you ration, you avail
And flow instantly to the seeker

1.27.6

Coerce the mortal
When he struggles, O flame
Coerce him with your sparkle
He will achieve dominance and fame

1.27.7

Fire of force
Inspired by the plenty with no refrain
Things in that creature you endorse
While in track on any plane

1.27.8

Fire, must you bring the army?
Along with strength that's universal
Wise seers keep it safe in this journey
Richness of plenty fulfills the goal

1.27.9

Fire, wake up to this flatter
Even to Rudra, your position
Form all persons, their sacrifices matter
Your hymn packed with vision

1.27.10

Fire, may you be great with no bound
Passionate in every perception
Extensive and full of charm
May your favors amplify our conception

1.27.11

Full of spontaneity is our master
A divine perception awakens
Listen to us, our fuel of many a prayer
A flame you are, burn into prominence

1.27.12

Bowing to great gods, prayers to the lesser
Curtsy to young, respect to old, keen n' swift
A sacrifice most for all gods, make it better
You elder gods make the self-expression lift

1.27.13

Angirasa

Agni, first of the Angirasa came forth
Seer, a friend of gods, of their benevolence
From your own actions, a seer, you took birth
Knowledge, enacted by Marut of glowing arms

1.31.1

The first fire, to Angirasa, it's special
Seer! An endeavor, the gods started
Festooned at that level
Covering all sides, nothing discarded

In many ways they express you
For the earthlings you appear wise
Span across the world of two
In man, you dwell in many ways

1.31.2

O fires, to the thinker, decreed
Heaven lies within reach of few
To the grieving man with good deed
Now he does good motivated by you

Released you were by an agitation
When heaven and earth combined
It positioned you in a higher station
Established you in the other behind

1.31.4

O Agni, sprinkle knowledge, nurture
Mantras admire you, thoughts are clear
Sole fire, from every direction proffer
Knowledge for all. First, illumine this seeker

1.31.5

A mortal you create with laws of immortal
Hearing the divine inspiration everyday
Agni, the wise yearns two-fold lives of normal
Happiness and pleasure, you induce, anyway

1.31.7

Exceptional knowledge of the fire, the cue
Your protection imparts strength and cure
Wealth and heroism abundant in you
Undeniable you are. Law of work stays secure

1.31.10

Among those born, the gods made you first
Fire, king of every man
My sibling, Agni sought birth, he coerced
He was Ila, the visionary word for man

1.31.11

Agni guards the fiery nectar
Fortifies the body, successors and cattle too
A defending knight, an offering to the altar
Safe are the layers, the mantra, grounded into

1.31.12-1.31.13

Calm Agni, the music setter
Excellent are the valuables. Supreme is He
Weak⁹ turns the heap of shelter
Revered father cooks for the wise for free

1.31.14

---

⁹Aadhrasya – weak; chit – heap, pramati - protection

Agni grants south to the human
Moves to the right, an armor in a bag[10]
Spreads joy[11] through a savory meals fusion
Loves every creature, promises heaven his flag

1.31.15

Manu's fiery taste[12], Angira and Yayati enjoy
Seated[13] are sages through a clean and pure feat
Pure[14], deliver the deities' offspring[15] in joy
From outside, bring the Yaksa a seat

1.31.16-1.31.17

And, Agni with Apah knows the divine
With strength, oversee the cyclical cognition
Ancient wealth increases upstream
Stealthily[16] hastened, strengthened mission

1.31.18

Kanva

Agni, such words in hymns, we supplicate
Head of families who serve many a deity
Men on winning Agni make him their strength
Remain everyone's helper, be excellent today

1.36.1-1.36.2

You, our messenger, our priest mighty
Mighty flames spread, reach the blue
Enkindled by Varuna, Mitra, Aryaman three
Mortal gains wealth, pours offerings on you

1.36.3-1.36.4

---

[10]Sayutam – A bag
[11]SyonakRit – One who spreads happiness
[12]ManuSwadAgne – Manu's taste is fiery
[13]Sadan - seat
[14]AchA - pure
[15]Yahu - child
[16]Tasang – stealthy, crawl like an animal. Srj – rush, hurled, let go. Sumat (along with or together). Vajavat – being strong.

O priest, bring in the cheer
Head of the house, men's messenger
Declarations by the deities and seer
Converge in you, grouped together

1.36.5

In auspicious Agni, gifts we offer
Grace every day, let us beget heroic sons
In his own splendor, this devout prayer
Kindle Agni with gifts, rule the opponents

1.36.6-1.36.7

Vritra, they beat, slew; he couldn't hide
Made the sky of earth, heaven a wide abode
Glorious Bull, invoked, stood by Kanva's side
Steeds neighing for kin they behold

1.36.8

Take a seat, mighty, shiny
Entertainer of every deity
The sacred food sits worthy
Agni, please loosen the smokey
Bear Manu's offerings ordained by deity

Kanva, Medhatithi, Vrisan, Upastuta four
Wealth, in plenty, they afford

1.36.9-1.36.10

Medhatithi and Kanva, Agni they kindle again
Songs of praise, for his power they sing
His wealth perfect, he joins the deities' wing
Another offering to the fire king

1.36.11-1.36.12

Like Savitr, will he lend some aid?
Will he give strength, our call runs unafraid
Save us from trouble, will he stand erect?
Flame, will he burn the demons to death?

1.36.13-1.36.14

Raise us, we may live and commute
Among the deities, you sense our faith
Save us, Agni, from the difficult brute
Save us from malice and what's incorrect

1.36.15

Save us from one who would injure or slay
Young you are, you blaze a lofty light
Punch with a club, let your fiery teeth play
Smite the wicked, left and right

Let no man plot against us this night
Let no brute prevail or drown us in fright

1.36.16

Agni gives Kanva felicity n' power
Helps friends *Medhatithi* and *Upastuta* win
Summons *Ugradeva, Yadu, Turvasa* from far
Navavastva, Brihadratha, Turviti beat the foe to ruin

1.36.17-1.36.18

Hey Agni, Manu established you a light
For the needs of humankind
Sprung from law, for *Kanva* you burn bright
That's Agni, people admire and befriend

1.36.19

Dreary sweeps Agni's flames of splendor
Approach not, don't intervene
Agni, devour every demon and sorcerer
Consume that devouring fiend

1.36.20

Kanva

Agni, Jataveda, immortal you are
For Usha, your many-hued, glowing gift
Our chants float to morning deities afar
Assured by Ashvin, famed Usha acts swift

1.44.1-1.44.2

Agni, today's messenger from heaven
Foggy, the light from the morning rite
Noble, young n' dear to charitable men
Jataveda, bring deities to a dawn of bright

1.44.3-1.44.4

You, Agni, I extol; you're so dear
Deathless nourisher of this world
Immortal you are, offerings you bear
At the sacrifice, best and bold

1.44.5

Speak nice who praise with their hymn
Young deity, worshipped, honey-tongued
Praskanva - a longer life awaits him
Will he honor a heavenly front?

1.44.6

Let the crowd view Agni kindled as priest
Agni, bring with speed the deities and wise
Usha, Savitr, Ashvin, Bhaga, Agni at dawn or night
Fair is the rite, Soma poured to Kanva's allies

1.44.7-1.44.8

Agni presides over our sacrifice tonight
Agni, our trusted messenger
Bring the deities who at dawn view the light
Bring them to savor the Soma nectar

1.44.9

Agni shines, past dawns still crimson
As Manu, we request you perform the rite
Deities' high priest, fulfill every mission
Your flame like floods roar most bright

1.44.10-1.44.12

No rest, every deity you escort these days
Find Mitra, Aryaman a seat to join the rite
Lawmakers, caregivers, Marut-s, hear our praise
Varuna, Ashvin, Usha, enjoy Soma tonight

1.44.13-144.14

Vasu-s, Rudra-s, Aditya-s, need Agni's revere
Offspring's of Manu, they know the fair rite
They pour blessings down, can you hear?
Bring thirty-three deities to the site

1.45.1-1.45-2

Jataveda[17], hear Praskanva's[18] call
Atri, Virupa, Angira seek Priyamedha's ear
Calls on Agni, Priyamedha's sons, them all
Agni's rules holy rites with his blazing fire

1.45.3-1.45.4

Eulogy for the fire restored with holy oil
Kanva's sons seek Agni's aid in swift
His domicile fame, they recall
They call Agni, his hair aflame, to bear a gift

1.45.5-1.45.6

Balladeers sing for Agni, the herald priest
Pressing Soma for Agni, rush to the feast
His light blazes on the mortal priest
When they bring him the sacred gift

1.45.7-1.45.8

Son of strength, take a seat on the sacred grass
With deities at early morn, sip the Soma juice
Joint invocations, Agni, you are a celestial class
Yesterday, deities sipped Soma in profuse

1.45.9-1.45.10

Goutam Nodha

Never timorous, he is Vivasvan's herald
On many a path, most excellent
He measures mid-regions instead
His service to the deities is heaven-sent

1.58.1

---

[17] An attribute of Agni with Agni's association to true knowledge
[18] Praskanva belongs to the Kanva clan of Rishis

No decay, he knows the fuel, of course
Eagerly on dry wood he spreads even
His back, sprinkled, glistens like a horse
Loud he blusters to the heights of heaven

1.58.2

Higher than Vasu-s and Rudra-s reach
The lord of riches, seated as high priest
He rushes in a car to every living thing
Delay he doesn't, gives boons a boost

1.58.3

Roused by wind, spreads he, in dry wood
His sickle tongue lets out a mighty roar
Dark runs Agni, where glitters the waves
A bull, he charges towards the treetop core

1.58.4

Enflamed his teeth from a wind to bear
Hastens he, in woods, a bull among cows
Bright strength drifts to everlasting air
Fixed and moving, he soars and plows

1.58.5

Brighu-s establish you among their men
A treasure, beauteous, easy to raise
You, Agni, a herald, a guest from heaven
An auspicious friend in the celestial race

1.58.6

Agni, seven-tongued, the priests elect
Vasu-s herald serves me riches, I serve food
Grants me a refuge with no defect
Saves man's stress from an iron fortitude

1.58.7-1.58.8

Agni, be a refuge, bright one
Be a shelter to the singer
Misery, let the singer have none
Enrich the singer with quick prayer

1.58.9

Gifts, for Brighu[19], Maatarisvan[20] spread
Brighu, a child of two births, in a swift envoy
To obey this ruler, deities and men unafraid
A priest, he takes his seat at the break of day

1.60.1-1.60.2

The heart-born, many praises they freight
Praise for him his tongue honeyed-sweet
For him, mortal priests and men create
A delicate lunch; a succulent treat

1.60.3

Purifier friend to man, priest to behold
Agni, a friend fends the riches of delight
To Agni, Gautama's sing hymns and extol
Decked on a horse, he arrives quick and bright

1.60.4

Parasara

Track you, must the bards?
A thief, you lurk in a cave with stolen rays
A mere worship, you give to the gods
Satiated are the holy ones by your praise

1.65.1

Ways of a divine law, the deities tread
A gathering vast as heaven
Celestial waters praise the growing babe
Born in a womb, law seats beckon

1.65.2

A food, a habitat, a hill, a stream
A steed urged to run in swift canter
The Sindhu[21] rivers rushing
None to check his course, none to anchor

1.65.3

---

[19] Brighu, Gautama – members of the clan
[20] Maatarisvan – Sometimes an ally of Agni, or even Agni himself
[21] Sindhu, mispronounced Indu or Indus is a long stretch of river

A brother to sister, a flood does he set
As a king eats the rich, he devours the wood
Urged by winds, in the forest, his spread
Agni shears earth's hair to its root

1.65.4

A swan, he skirts the flood
With the wise in mind, he wakes at morn
Sage like Soma, sprung from law like a bud
Mighty, shining far, young Agni is born

1.65.5

Sun's glances vary in wealth
Like breath of life, like the breed
A swift bird, a cow yields milk in stealth
Pure, refulgent, to the woods in speed

1.66.1

Safe in a pleasant home, tucked
Like ripened corn, will he conquer men
Famed among folks, a seer at laud
A friendly steed, he vouchsafes then

1.66.2

Flame, insatiate with eternal might
Caring for all, a lady at home
Bright is his shine, pale with folks in sight
A golden car heading to a fight alone

1.66.3

He strikes in terror like a dart
An archer's arrow tipped in flame
Master of future and present at that
Maidens' lover, Matrons' lord, the same

1.66.4

Will he lead our ways? May we attain god?
As cows reach their shelter at dusk
Floods of flames, he shoots a squad
Rays rise to the heaven of trust

1.66.5

Victory in woods, respect of a king so dear
Gracious like peace, he is full of thought
Bent in a cavern, he strikes gods with fear
Men sing him prayers looped in a knot

1.67.1-1.67.2

Unborn, he sustains a broad earth above
His effective utterance fixes the sky
Agni protects spots that cattle love
From a den he moves to a nest held high

1.67.3

Who knows his dwelling in a nest
Approaches the stream of holy law
Who releases him, chanting sacred rites
To them, he promises wealth with no flaw

1.67.4

Growing in herbs, within every mother
Every child will she bear
Wise to men in waters' home of another
The wise build for him a significant chair

1.67.5

Blending, restless, ascending the sky
Unveils he the nights and what stands or moves
In greatness, among other gods who sit high
Dominant, a sole deity, he proves

1.68.1

Men turn joyful in your power
From dry wood you are born
Your lordship, they share at this hour
Eternal law, in familiar ways, they adorn

1.68.2

Lawful thoughts at law's bidding
All work performed, he quickens the portion
Reflecting on self, fortunes he's defending
Gifts for them, who offer oblation

1.68.3

Manu's clan sits with you, a priest in time
Among all treasures, he alone is superior
Men yearn for children to stretch their line
Disappointments are never a barrier

1.68.4

His word, they hear; his wish, fulfil their ardor
As sons obey their commander's request
Rich food, unbars his wealth, like a door
He decks the heaven's vault in a starry nest

1.68.5

Bright is he, splendid as Usha's lover
Streams two joined worlds with a heavenly light
Born with might, he offers them cover
As the father of deities, whose sons despite

1.69.1

Humble fire discerns the rays below
Like the sweet taste of food
For men in the fragment of bliss lies the glow
Seated gracious in an asylum for good

1.69.2

Domicile born, a lovely, pleasing son
A strong steed, he bears on the owner
When heroes I call upon
Agni, you gain much divine power

1.69.3

None dare break these laws of yours
When you listen to many a chief
In your boast, you strike your peers
From disgrace, only you bring relief

1.69.4

Usha's lover springs a light to pour
Hued is the morning, does he remember me?
Bearing themselves, they unbar the door
All ascend to the heaven's marquee

1.69.5-1.69.9

Surplus food by prayer, only the modest win
Agni's fair light pervades such an act
He observes laws made in heaven
And laws, mortal man must adapt

1.70.1

He germinates water and wood
Sprouts spring up, stay still or move
Immortal is he; he cares for the good
On this rock, in the house, him we approve

1.70.2

Rays swing from woods, a tribute to light
Men part as they part with family cash
Agni heralds with light, an archer to a fight
Fierce avenger in a fight, he plays fiery rash

1.70.3

Who serves Agni, earns riches n' gold
Fire endorsed by dawn and night, sits in light
Like a brave archer, skilled and bold
Agni, a fierce avenger, shines in a fight

1.70.4-170.6

He, the loving, earns love of a spouse
Many hues he sets, bright, dark, and red too
Angirasa's fortress safe with a roar to douse
Way to heaven paved in beams of morning blue

1.71.1-1.71.2

Order, they create to make his services adaptive
Giving to yearning folks who act loyal
They feel no thirst, they arrive active
Sweet food for gods, they bolster no denial

1.71.3

Maatarisvan once stirred the fire
In every house, he grows bright and gallant
Brighu, he and I, as friends aspire
To royalty on a commission, balanced

1.71.4

Man poured syrup for the heaven
Free became Father from a close encounter
Archer boldly shot him with an arrow then
The god threw his splendor on his daughter

1.71.5

Who lights flames for you in their home?
Who offers prayers daily, which you love most
Will you increase his affluence alone?
Who incites you, whose riches do you boast?

1.71.6

Awaits Agni, a sacrificial foot in quiver
Just as seven mighty rivers meet the sea
The food, our siblings fail to discover
Care with the gods is the key

1.71.7

Light fills the men's lord to a brim
From heaven descends a clear vapor
Agni brings to light, full of spirit again
A young host, blameless neighbor

1.71.8

Swift as thought, its journey
Sun, alone is the lord of bounty
Varuna and Mitra, fair handed king's army
Precious nectar from a new foundry

1.71.9

Agni, break not this ancestral bond
Sage with deep knowledge
Old age, dark cloud, ruins the body beyond
Before trouble alights, save this wretch

1.71.10

Wise bow humble to a gift
Everchanging Agni gives an immortal gift
Deities search for flame, who with us on feet
Weary, they arrive at Agni's asylum in swift

1.72.1-1.72.2

Holy oil for Agni and the pure
They serve in three autumn seasons
Divine names and icons speed the cure
Bodies turn to grace with reasons

1.72.3

Earth and heaven know them
In Rudra[22] powers, the sages invest
A mortal band keeps a safe distance
Finds fire standing in the lofty nest

1.72.4

With spouses they attempt toward
Kneeling before him in a paid laud
Friends find within, a friend's eye to guard
Craft own bodies, the chaste steward

1.72.5

The holy stay back to expose
In your thrice-seven mystic panel
One-minded preserve Amrita[23]; they enclose
Guard the life of their plants and cattle

1.72.6

Agni, you know our work
Our lives dangle on your supply of food
Will you join our diligent envoy network?
Skilled in the path of gods, pray don't collude

1.72.7

The law, seven strong floods of heaven
Pure in thought, discerns every rich gate
Sarama[24] hides in the cattle's strong prison
Where human race shelters instead

1.72.8

---

[22] Rudra is a terrifying figure among the deities. Read about the deities later
[23] Amrita is the nectar of immortality
[24] Sarama is a member of the clan

Noble deeds point to a life undying
In the Bird's aid, Aditi[25], her sons resume power
Heaven's eyes, the immortals gift him
Red steeds drift quick as the river

1.72.9-1.72.10

Satiated with food and riches, ready to lead
Cherished like a guest, his servants prosper
Like Savitr[26], staying true, his rule to heed
In a breath of joy, strive to win his power

1.73.1-1.73.2

King fenced by friends, he dwells on earth
He's a god who survives the evil douse
Heroes preside in safety set forth
A righteous girl dear to her spouse

1.73.3

Our men secure every dwelling
Flame pours splendor on a lavish affair
Rich, princely seeker wins food untiring
War booty, the gods win their share

1.73.4-1.73.5

Inflated laws radiant with divine engage
Will he ask a favor, a river to its beach?
O fire, in whose favor heavens praise the sage
Night 'n dawn, black n' purple their reach

1.73.6-1.73.7

Agni reveals riches in a world of three
He circles the world as her shadow
Can a race a steed with a steed in ecstasy?
Just men with men, hero with a hero

---

[25] Aditi, mother of 7 deities
[26] Savitr, another attribute of the sun. Read about the gods later

Wealth lord unfurled by fathers in present
Princes live past a hundred winters
Agni, are these hymns of praise pleasant?
Can we rein your steeds of rich glitters?

1.73.8-1.73.10

Rahugana Goutam

Down the sacrificial trail
We express the word and hymn
Our thoughts swing to Agni's prevail
Who listens without and within

1.74.1

Supreme, ancient, no fail
You are the first in a world of three
We gather Agni, pour the clear fuel
Our insights you guard for free

1.74.2

In verdict, all creatures dare speak
Vritra is dead, the fire burns at the core
His many conquests no more bleak
Bring out the wealth in every war

1.74.3

His messages, you, the fire take home
His offerings, you transport
On this arduous journey never alone
Path of the sacrifice now in effect

1.74.4

Complete is he, in every offer we make
Complete as the sacrifice source
Perfect, he is, among the gods awake
Angira, son of force

1.74.5

A rich delight to adjure
Two gods, bring them with you
What we express and endure
Offerings in their journey ensue

1.74.6

Heard is no tramp, no riot
But the horses still march their part
On a mission, moves the chariot quiet
Agni, you are ready to start

1.74.7

As fostered by you, the sire
Digressed not, is the horse of life
One will succeed the other, O fire
Sacrifice giver advances in his stride

1.74.8

Within the seeker and many a god
Within them, you dwell
Spreads a luminous cradle of energy broad
Agni, does your grace propel?

1.74.9

Gods, accept this hymn, a food o' delight
In your mouth, offerings we pour
Agni, best of Angirasa[27], hear a prayer this night
Among men, Agni, who is your kin for sure?

Whose worship is worth your adore
Whom do you rely? What folklore?

1.75.1-1.75.3

Agni, family of man, a beloved friend
A Friend, who friends can implore
In our sacrifice, will Mitra, Varuna[28] attend?
Agni, bring the gods home to our shore

1.75.4-1.75.5

---

[27] Agni, is a member of the Angirasa here. Angirasa is of the Kanva clan.
[28] Mitra, Varuna – Deities. Read more about the deities later

Can our mind go any near to please?
What hymn brings the best?
Who acquires your power from a sacrifice?
With what mind is this prayer addressed?

1.76.1

Come here Agni, as Hotra[29], a seat for you
You never deceive our leader
May three worlds in turn love you
Worship the gods and win their favor

1.76.2

Agni, will you burn the Rakshasa[30] fiend
From our sacrifice, will you ward every curse?
Will you bring Soma[31]'s inlets to stay redeemed?
Greetings to the bounteous giver of the universe

1.76.3

A priest invoked, offspring from his speech
Here, with the gods, have a seat
Tasked you are to cleanse and achieve
Awaken us, confer on us a wealth complete

1.76.4

Priests in the Manu[32] clan and you can weigh
A sage with sages to seek the gods
Now, truthful Agni, seek this day
Your joy-bestowing ladle clears the odds

1.76.5

Agni, can I make an offer?
What is a word so solemn?
What is the word for the gods you prefer?
What word I can chant to you, radiant one?

---

[29] Hotra in latter texts becomes associated with Agni as Agnihotra. Here he is an allied priest.

[30] Rakshasa is an enemy of the deities. Men fear their wild side.

[31] Soma is a sweet nectar, intoxicating, invigorating. Soma in later texts also represents a deity. Authors dedicate Book 9 to Soma.

[32] Manu, the first of men. In this case the head of the Kanva clan

Undying in mortals, the truth, you own
Priest, conduct the sacrifice of the higher
Will you fashion every god in every man?
How can I make an offer to the great fire?

1.77.1

In peace, covered in truth's high tier
In a sacrificial pilgrimage, you, the priest
Configures him with fire to many a prayer
By you, gods in mortals stay increased

He knows every kind
Adores them by the power of mind

1.77.2

The will, the strength, the powers within
As Mitra, you chauffeur only the great
Desiring the gods, the Arya[33] sings you a hymn
Will the sacrifice's rewards aggregate?

1.77.3

Agni, tough amid the strong
Words overwhelm the opposing force
Master of wealth; gods join this song
Thoughts with radiant powers enforce

1.77.4

Fire n' truth, he knows all things born
Gautama praises Agni by his hymn
Will Agni ignite his power with plenty to adorn
Harmony within grasp to rise above the dim

1.77.5

Nimble Jataveda, Goutam-s sing a tune
To you, as you are, a song for you to take
Seeking wealth, the Goutam-hymns wish a boon
Lauded are you for glories' sake

1.78.1-1.78.2

---

[33] Arya – A nobleman

47

Like Angira, we call on the winner of the spoil
Vritra slayer, which Dasyu[34] libel will you roil?
Rahugana[35]'s sons in a pleasant tune embroil
Laud your glories' in fuels of oil

1.78.3-1.78.5

Blatant in the mid world, in curls of gold
A raging serpent, rushes like the tempest
Pure bright, in the morning cold
Like chaste girls, true, active and reckless

1.79.1

Flash of a wing, strength his style
When the dark bull bellows around us
He arrives, the blessed turn to smile
Water pours, clouds turn thunderous

1.79.2

He streams with a milk of worship
Caressing a direct path of order alone
Aryaman, Mitra, Varuna, Parijman[36] join the trip
Where lies the nether press-stone

1.79.3

Jataveda[37], son of strength, please protect
Agni, kindled, good and wise
Exalted in this song, in this subject
Shine in many forms, shine in radiant highs

1.79.4-1.79.5

Shine by night until morning break
Rakshasa burns in your teeth so sharp
Adorable in our rites, Agni's uptake
When chanted is this hymn superb

1.79.6-1.79.7

---

[34] Dasyu like Rakshasa is another dreaded human foe
[35] Rahugana – a member of the Kanva clan
[36] Parijman is associated with the fire and the moon.
[37] Jataveda is an epithet of Agni. The all knowing attribute.

Agni, bring wealth of our choice
In every fight, no weakness, no redress
Promise us a wealthy grace to live n' rejoice
Grant us a favor to progress

1.79.8-1.79.9

Gautam desires bliss, he sings Agni a song
Sung with care to every pointed flame
Crooked man must fall who does us wrong
Be large, bring fortunes of your acclaim

Agni, keen and swift
Thousand eyes chase the Rakshas' far
By then he sings in thrift
The herald enjoys the lauds in his glare

1.79.10-1.79.12

Kritasa

Jataveda, this praise like a car, I record
Agni, confirm, we suffer no harm
For whom do you sacrifice, who will you reward?
He is now a hero, each foe a charm

Content like the moon, he waxes strong
Agni, ensure we suffer no harm

1.94.1-1.94.2

You, we kindle to fulfil every thought
In you, gods munch an offering served warm
Will you bring Aditya family to this spot?
Agni, confirm, we suffer no harm

1.94.3

More fuel, we bring, offerings to burn
Reminding you of every festive juncture
Realize the thoughts, prolong our lives in turn
Agni, confirm, no harm shall we suffer

1.94.4

His moves of a vicar, a guardian rebel
Shielding every creature with rays running firm
Usha's herald, mighty and able
Agni, ensure we suffer no harm

1.94.5

High priest's work flows perfect
Shines bright, shines near, far, lovely his form
What you see even in the dark of night
Agni, ensure we suffer no harm

1.94.6-1.94.7

Top runs his car, potions pour out
Hymns triumph over evil n' their swarm
He attends spoken words then they sprout
Agni, ensure we suffer no harm

1.94.8

Strike evil with your weapon
Your car bridles four steeds red
In a sacrifice, give the singer his freedom
Roars as a bull, the car runs wind-swept

Smoke flagged car hits forests widespread
Agni, our ally, no harm, we crusade

1.94.9-1.94.10

At Agni's growl, terrified, the birds flee
Mitra and Varuna stay calm
Dousing Marut-s' wrath, their hearts agree
Friend Agni, ensure we suffer no harm

1.94.11-1.94.12

Friend of gods, Vasu of the Vasu clan
In your wide, safe net may we dwell
With Soma, turn benign, in your abode's span
Agni, friend, all harm, you silently quell

1.94.13-1.94.14

Eternal flame, grant him the rich
Make him free of every sin
Empower him to have children quick
Can I be his identical twin?

1.94.15

Agni, you know the good fortune
Elongate our days, may we live longer
Varuna, *Mitra*, *Aditi* grant us a new boon
Sindhu, Earth, Heaven, grant us the honor

1.94.16

Two unlike, a target they share
Each in succession nourishes an infant dear
One bears a tot, divine, golden debonair
Bright and fair in shine is the other pair

1.95.1

Ten daughters of Tvastar, wary and young
Make this infant, endure the quarters strong
Move around him, his flames flung long
Bright amid men, his glory they sing along

1.95.2

His birth of three they honor
In the waters, mid and heaven's border
Prevailing in the east on earth's banner
Seasons, he sets in a new order

1.95.3

How many know this secret of One?
Brought forth his Mothers, this brilliant son
Seeded from the waters, it blazed firm
Wise and great, always on the run

1.95.4

Turgid, bright, his instincts inborn
In her lap of waving waters, he plays along
Tvastar's two worlds dreaded as he was born
They turn to him, revere the mighty lion

1.95.5

Mother's instincts, the Two tend him
Bellowing cattle, cater to his every whim
Mighty is this lord, mighty his vim
Balm anointed to oblation with trim

1.95.6

Savitr[38] stretches his arms to grasp earth
The Two make him brilliant robes of worth
In a new form, milk and water pour forth
Deities meet, worship the sages curt

1.95.7-1.95.8

Wide flows strength by an expanse
Kindled Agni to preserve and enhance
In a desert, he makes steam, floods the lands
Owning the ancient; he moves in fresh plants

1.95.9-1.95.10

With fuel to nourish Agni's fury
Blazes auspiciously in his glory
Varuna, Mitra, Aditi grant this enquiry
Sindhu, Earth, Heaven also grant this story

1.95.11

In ancient ways, with power did he rise
Straight, he absorbed all that was wise
Water and bowl gave him a friendly guise
Gods in wealth conferred on Agni likewise

1.96.1

A call from the past
Progeny of men get their being and caste
Light so bright, heaven waters soar fast
Agni gave then the deities wealth amassed

1.96.2

---

[38] Savitr is an Aditya, sometimes an attribute of Surya

Praise for his toil, folks of Arya clan
Maatarisvan's[39] offspring in the isle of man
Folks, 'n Father of two worlds safe in his plan
When Agni gave, wealth, the deities began

1.96.3-1.96.4

Night n' dawn exchange hues henceforth
Feeding the infant shining on heaven and earth
His roots in wealth; roots in life, its eternal worth
Agni gave; deities built all the wealth

1.96.5-1.96.6

Between new and an old habitat of wealth
A mansion is born, it came before time
Guarding what is, what will come forth
Deities enjoy wealth, Agni conferred to prime

1.96.7

Give wealth, help us conquer the asset
Give wealth with champs for us to beget
Give wealth, food 'n offspring, don't you forget
Give wealth, length of days for you to set

1.96.8

Invigorated with fuel, Agni, makes the pure
Blazes in a glory we can only savor
Varuna and Mitra grant our prayer
Aditi, Sindhu, Earth, Heaven grant us a favor

1.96.9

On us, shine wealth, chase the vile away
To harvest, home, wealth, we sacrifice, we pray
His praise for our chiefs who sacrifice anyway
Let his light vanquish evil everyday

1.97.1-1.97.3

---

[39] Maatarisvan was the first to bring Agni to humankind.

May devotees, sons and I stay alive
Winning light beams reach every side
Turns every side your face, jubilant you arrive
May your light chase evil before they thrive

1.97.4-1.97.6

His vision covers every direction fast
Takes us past our foes in a raft
In the raft, sails us over the flooded path
May his light chase every evil's wrath

1.97.7-1.97.9

Vaisvanara, we seek your grace
You reign over every living race
Sprung to life, you scan the first place
Vaisvanara's rivalry with Surya to retrace

1.98.1

Agni lodges in heaven and earth
Permeating trees on the ground, he sets forth
Agni's and Vaisvanara's vigor have no dearth
Fields us day 'n night from every rival worth

1.98.2

Point your truth, Vaisvanara on us
Let abundant wealth gather round us
Varuna and Mitra grant this prayer of ours
Aditi, Sindhu, Earth and Heaven hear thus

1.98.3

Kashyap

Proposed is Soma for fire
He who remembers his every birth
Rescind he will for sure
The awareness of our foes, their wealth

Fire paves the line to the joy crushing grief
Carting us safely on a raft on a river of mischief

1.99.1

Dirghatama

Agni by the altar in a shelter's comfort
He enjoys food I fetch in his place of birth
Hymns cloak the bright one in a coat
In a lit car, he dispels despair from earth

1.140.1

Twice born, thrice, he gulps food in full
In an instant, what he ate grows again
With mouth and tongue of a noble bull
He, an elephant, eats plants n' grain

1.140.2

A pair in the dark stir each other
Both parents rush to the child
Wild his tongue, destroying cutter
Under watch, we cherish him as wild

1.140.3

For every man, reined is the steed
Running light, it ploughs to blacken the line
Harsh is its fleet, glides in easy speed
Sped by the wind, rapid, it runs blind

1.140.4

He dispels horrors of a dark gloom
Glorious turns the show, flames fly forth
On a spacious tract he throws a fume
Panting, the thunder roars abrupt

1.140.5

Rushes to a tree, the Bull must confirm
Showing his valor among many a woman
Decorates the glory of his form
Shakes his horn, the naughty demon

1.140.6

Covered, yet with no cover
Clutching, he finds a place to rest
When they wax, they profit from divine power
Merge to shape as parents unexpressed

1.140.7

Girls with long tresses rush to his embrace
Dead is he to rise again to meet them alive
Loud he roars, frees them from old age
Filling them with a new spirited life

1.140.8

Licking mother's cloak, he visits far and wide
Wanders the fields where beasts flee brisk
Supports the blackened path in every stride
Licks as he moves, he roams quick

1.140.9

Along with wealthy chiefs, will you shine?
Snort will you, a Bull in a familiar home
Cast every cherubic wrap to blaze alone
How you wear a new coat in a combat zone?

1.140.10

May these perfect prayers endear
Unlike an imperfect word that only please
Brilliance stems from your form in clear
Wont you grant us wealth with ease?

1.140.11

Grant wealth to chariots at our homes
Agni, give a frenzied boat its moving feet
More wealth for our wealthy princes
And for all folks, we seek refuge in that treat

1.140.12

In this laud, your consent we yearn
May the three worlds and flowing water
Bestow long life, cattle and corn
May ruddy Usha's choices cater

1.140.13

He sprang from force, he failed to dim
Founded a new brilliance of the lord
At his liking, prolific echoes the hymn
Songs of sacrifice fetch and flow toward

1.141.1

Superb, enduring, he dwells in food
In seven mothers, he rests, his dwelling place
Fearing what may drain Bull's riches of good
Maidens bring him a tenth's offering of grace

1.141.2

From depths of time, from a Steer's form
Men of power defined him; vigor controlled
Hidden rub, Maatarisvan pilots the transform
A blend of sweet drink in the days of old

1.141.3

He alights from the Highest father
Among plants, he ascends hungry, amazed
Hastening his birth, the Two try to foster
In youth, he assumes birth, his light ablaze

1.141.4

Arrives, he with Mothers in gold
Pure, intact, he sprouts in size and power
First is his rise, vigorous from the old
Next is his run, amid the younger and lower

1.141.5

Made him a herald at a morning rite
Demanded of him as Bhaga to pour favors
Praised by the deities will, in the power of might
He borrows a drink from mortal neighbors

1.141.6

How did the holy one rise? Urged by the gust?
Winding like a snake in the wild, dry grass
Why, he converts everything to dust
Black-winged, pure of birth, walks several paths

1.141.7

Unique craftsmen make a chariot swift
With limbs of red, leaps he into the heavens
Devotees loom in shades of black n' bright
Rapid flies their strength to a hero's violence

1.141.8

Agni, Varuna stands guard to an eternal law
Mitra and Aryaman become strong
As the rim holds spokes in its claw
With your valor, you embrace them all along

1.141.9

Agni toils, he has an offer
To his abode, wealth and gods walk along
To Agni as Bhaga, we renew this honor
To the rich, child of strength is our battle-song

1.141.10

Promise us riches, let their worth unfold
In this shelter, blessed and awed
Promise us wealth to direct the world
Let the wise rein a sacrificial assent from god

1.141.11

Splendid priest, listen to our cries
Priest in a radiant car travelling at rapid speed
May that Agni priest, ever wise
Steer us to bliss of the highest creed

1.141.12

Forceful hymns for Agni festoon our laud
Our prayers crown him as universal king
With wealthy chiefs, we configure a squad
Like the Sun over dark clouds forms a ring

1.141.13

Agni, to you I gift a fresh, robust hymn
My words, my song to the son of strength
Water born Agni, conveys every precious thing
On this season, the invoking priest rules earth

1.143.1

The day, Agni's birth at the highest plane
Maatarisvan learnt of the miracle infant
That day he kindled and enflamed
Heaven and earth, he spun brilliant

1.143.2

With age, flames decay not, stay on bright
Fair beams shine pretty, Agni's rays
Active light force, glimmers sleepless at night
Ageless he remains, like flooded days

1.143.3

Agni sent home with a simple hymn
Same Agni rules Varuna's worth
Agni possesses all, but the Brighu team
Though they took him to center of earth

1.143.4

No force dares stop him, not Maruts' roar
Dart sent out, a bolt from heaven
Agni's honed jaws chew trees n' devour
Like a warrior smiting his foes again

1.143.5

Will Agni enjoy our praise?
Vasu grants a wish, rinses us in wealth
Inspirer hastens our prayer; we gain a raise
His radiant glint, I extol; a song I've spelt

1.143.6

When you kindle, Agni turns a friend
His face seeped in oil, sponsors the Law
Bright in our rallies, keen and inflamed
Clad in light, he lifts hymns with no flaw

1.143.7

Surround us in safety, in your fortitude
With guards auspicious and strong
Guards never sleep, sensible, always good
Keep children away from the wrong

1.143.8

A priest commits to a sacrifice
A glorious hymn floats alight
He meets ladles turning right in concise
They kiss where he abides in delight

1.144.1

For him, law streams as a song
Held at home in the birthplace of the lord
He resides at the waters' lap; moves along
Absorbed in divine powers, adored

1.144.2

In turns, the Two strive to a shared end
A beauteous form, they attempt to gain
Like Bhaga, we invoke, which he'll depend
He drives the car, grips the horse's rein

1.144.3

Furnished by Two from the same abode
Night as in day, born gray, fleeting age
Animate ten fingers, pieties for this lord
He speeds a slope of deeds with a sage

1.144.4-1.144.5

Agni, a herdsman, in his own might
Rules heaven and earth by his drive
The Mighty Two, gold and bright
Roll on the sacred grass to arrive

1.144.6

Agni, accept with joy this prayer
Give joy, your birth is from the holy law
Turn every side with your eyes fair
House stuffed with pleasant food, but raw

1.144.7

They implore him, packed with wisdom
Every rebuke crowds every command
Lord of strength, to our thoughts does he come
Power lord is he, strength advanced

1.145.1

They ask, but grasp not the Agni mind's sway
He recollects the past and future alright
Ladles n' mares for him, he cares what I say
Still a babe, a nimble victor, a spirited might

1.145.2-1.145.3

He clasps all he meets to renew his run
A newborn creeps forward with kin
Stirs weary folks to realms of joy and fun
Arrives in time to gifts that await him

1.145.4

Wild he runs in floods and forest
He rests on the highest podium
Unclogs the tradition to a conformist
Wise Agni, a True Law's custodian

1.145.5

Glory to a seven-rayed, triple-headed fiery fill
Agni, pure in his parents' heart
Reclines in laps of what moves, what stays still
Heaven turns bright with his support

1.146.1

Great seer grew under care, parents both
Sublime, unmoved by past, he goes far
Plants his feet firm on ridges of broad earth
Red flames lick the udders clear

1.146.2

Two visit their common fiery child
Shaped fair, his range goes everywhere
Gauging what path to travel
Entrusting desire to the Lord's care

1.146.3

Astute folks take him home quicker
Guard the ever young who has many a skill
Longing, they turn to look at the river
Look at the visible Sun most men fulfill

1.146.4

Noble, his birth in many a region
Pleading lives, great and small
Far, Agni in wealth, spreads to the foreign
Sires everyone in this progeny, short or tall

1.146.5

The aspiring, radiant, what do they bring?
Do they improve lives to make a difference?
Agni nurtures the seed and the offspring
Deities know joy in the holy law's deliverance

1.147.1

Mark my speech, stay ablaze
Some hate, others sing you with praise
Blind Mamateya's sight fixed by guardian rays
Pious preserved, foes' malice, a mere phrase

1.147.2-1.147.3

Will you punish the evil offender?
Double-tongued mortal who triggers harm
Save him from evil, whose lauds are a surrender
Hope there's no trouble, disease, or a storm

1.147.4-147.5

Maatarisvan pierced, he rubbed the fire
Gods messaged by that fire rush to combine
Agni set on the human pyre
Pleasant is his hue, pretty is his shine

1.148.1

No harm comes to him who praises you
Such is my praise. My help, do you approve?
I act to accept the good
Song from a singer who presents a salute

1.148.2

Steady in the car seat, hitched to nimble steed
He gives his word for bearers lead him bold
Chewing, crunched in the wood
Archer's wind shaft shoots a flame of gold

1.148.3-1.148.4

Hostile these men, blind, no foresight
Try to hurt the unborn child
Hope they never injure or stir a fright
Lovers save him from the world of wild

1.148.5

He hastens to give treasures kept at brink
Pressing stones, serve him when he speeds by
Seer Agni. In earth n' heaven's streams we drink
He hastens to the altar to rest. Him, we deify

1.149.1-1.149.2

He lights up a castle with joy and fun
Runs like a steed in a cloudscape of heaven
Agni, bright as the Sun
Hundredfold he exists in even

1.149.3

Twice born, he spreads the luster
Speeds by three luminous realms of azure
Goes past every region in this cluster
Best priest, he sacrifices where waters gather

1.149.4

Twice born priest, he knows what to keep
His love of glory, he stores everything
In his choice, considers nothing cheap
Who brings him gifts earns a noble offspring

1.149.5

Can I summon you Agni with special gift?
Break not the laws of a great inciting lord
Agni won't budge to aid the atheist
Who offers none. Even the wealthy barred

1.150.1-1.150.2

Splendid singer, that man
Great among singers in heaven
Agni, make us a principal when you can
With your worshippers, you can reckon

1.150.3

Mantras in etheric vacuity, imperishable are they
Where seated are gods in paradise
One who knows not, this learning is fake
The wise know this in concise

1.164.39

Agastya

Fire, lead us on a path to blessedness
Good manifests in what you teach
Detach the devious charm of wickedness
To you is this total surrender of speech

1.189.1

Praise to Agni as he leads us to bliss
Beyond plights, with no effort
Can you suggest a wide, joyous home that fits?
Grant our children, peace and comfort

1.189.2

Agni, for my maladies your cure is worth
Help me fight the hostile, they who despise
Help me in an effortless return to earth
Along with immortal gods, master of sacrifice

1.189.3

Defend us unceasing
Young Agni, forever shine within
Let this poet with no fear sing
Mighty fire, let fear not beset him again

1.189.4

Fire, protect us from evil, beast and reptile
From the many voracious, malefic fates
Mighty fire, these beasts are vile
Protect us from harm n' disgrace

1.189.5

Agni, a singer wears your armor, an equal
Fire, you were born of truth
No harm to the singer, no upheaval
Challenge the cheaters uncouth

1.189.6

Agni, how you set such groups apart
You contact a seeker at the right hour
Telling him where to start
Master of sacrifice, all pervading you are

1.189.7

Agni, son of mantra, friendly knight
These prayers, these secrets uncouple
In Rik mantras, thousands are the delight
An urge to smash the hour of struggle

1.189.8

Gritsamada

Agni's birth bathed in glowing light
Born from stone and water
Born from forest, terrestrial plant despite
Pure is his birth, human race master

2.1.1

Agni, hear this call, an offer across
Purity you define in the sacrifice order
A source of gloss
To a seeker of truth, will you tend his fire

Pilgrim of rite, your word, I have read
In our homes, you are the pastor head

2.1.2

Agni, among all, you are Indra, the bull
You are Vishnu who moves wide
Master of the word, you are Brahma in full
Respects to you, who knows the riches inside

Fire sustain us, keeps a close watch
Along with the goddess of sundry thought

2.1.3

Agni, you are Varuna, the king
With your hands, you uphold the law of work
You are Mitra, the potent, the desirable thing
You are Aryaman, lord of creatures that embark

Unparalleled in pleasures, Ana you are
Give a slice of knowledge from your rich reservoir

2.1.4

Agni, Tvashtar you are, infinite
For you, the seeker stocks with much force
Goddesses of energy is yours, friendly light
A natural oneness is what you endorse

You gallop fast and broad
Relish the powerful steed
You host every god
The amassed riches are great indeed

2.1.5

Agni, you are Rudra, heavens are a might
An army of life-gods are at your assembly
Loom over the desires flight
Go with the Usha's red winds nimbly

Delighted are we with you
You are Pushan, defending your crew

2.1.6

Agni, your offer of wealth so kind
The man knows what to labor
You are divine Savitri, you founded delight
Master of man, Bhaga, riches are your power

At an asylum, its guardian stalwart
Seekers revere you with work of worth

2.1.7

Men turn to you, domestic fire and master
You they crown, the intelligent king thence
Potent force of fire, everything you master
Move to thousands, hundreds and tens

2.1.8

Fire, their sacrifices adore you as father
That you may be their brother
When they see success no other
At the sacrificial work they seek another
The body with your light glows to distend
You are a son to a man
Man's blissful friend
From antagonists, offer us protection

2.1.9

Fire, you are artisan Rbhus, you work close
Act of surrender is your worship precise
Master of plenty, spread light on the treasure trove
Instruct us on insights of a sacrifice

2.1.10

Divine fire, Aditi you are, an undivided mother
You are Bharati, voice of submission
Grow by a word light as feather
You are Ila of hundred winters in unison

Discerned by the will of the wise in ardent
As Sarasvati, you slay the evil serpent

2.1.11

Agni, borne by us, in our horizons you expand
Glory and beauty cast a desirable hue
And they set your perfect visionary band
In the vastness, your abundance gets renewed

Abundance to arrive at the end of our ways
Your many riches span every place

2.1.12

When Aditi's sons designed fire as mouth
Pure gods transformed you into a tongue
Seekers empty on you their offer of truth
The gods feed on them in turn

2.1.13

Immortal, benefic gods engage
Feed on the offering made onto fire
From Agni's mouth, mortals sip the beverage
Pure is his birth from earth's matter

2.1.14

Agni, born perfect, with the gods you are
Leading them, often surpassing them
Your greatness pervades afar
In the worlds of earth and heaven

2.1.15

Those who chant on you get a gift
The wise will set them free
You lead us, our wealth pulled by your steed
To riches of a greater degree

Braced by heroes, may our voices in the vast
Set the coming of knowledge amassed

2.1.16

Ignite the fire of knowledge and teach
With sacrifice grow the creature and beast
Praise him with your offer, body and speech
Praise Surya, the summoned priest

He, heaven dweller, charioteer in our fights
In the kindling fire strong are the delights

2.2.1

Night and dawn speak in your ears
A cow moos at a calf in their enclosure
You travel heavens through man's years
Come on sparkle, the nights not yet over

2.2.2

Gods sent him into a world in the middle
Great worker, pilgrim of earth and heaven
Dashing his flaming chariot with a sizzle
Fire, our lauds to a friend within friend

2.2.3

Crooked they are, they pour the rain
Radiant he shines, gold in his light
In the etheric mid region
In his own habitat, inside

Defend mother, dappled she's become
Awaken us to knowledge
With your visionary eyes awaken them
You protect our births path at edge

2.2.4

Fire, as priest attend to this call
Your presence around every pilgrim-rite
With the Word, men crown, offer him all
Frolicking in fires, in his gold tiara bright

A heaven with stars of gold
Knows our steps in the terrestrial world

2.2.5

Agni. Your kindling. Our peace
In the light within, bring the gift of rich
Earth and heaven, a journey masterpiece
Offerings to gods, their moves you pitch

2.2.6

Agni, with vast possessions we seek
Thousand-fold riches entice us
Open the copious gates to a world of mystic
Earth and heaven defined thus

Just by the word, which has no second
Dawn breaks into Sun's brilliant world

2.2.7

Beautiful march the dawns, in a fiery parade
In roseate splendor, that march, he breaks
A different world of the Sun's crusade
Fire as pilgrim-rite, effective turn it takes

From man's vocal offer
You are king of man, his charming boarder

2.2.8

Pristine fire, what the thoughts allow
The human effects in gods
Then thoughts extend to benevolent cow
She will spare her milk in their combats

You speed them on their journey
Where occur many forms, many a bounty

2.2.9

Agni's warhorse, his heroic power
Awaken us to knowledge, unknown to man
Just the Word to lighten the high tower
Sacrosanct as the world of Sun

2.2.10

Awaken, Agni, you heard our laud
In you, there comes a birth
Born are bright seers unflawed
They run a swift race on earth

Agni, sacrifice you are
Swift steeds come to your service
Agni shines there as a radiant fire
In his own home, in Sun's furnace

2.2.11

Agni knows everyone born
He defines a peace, we must abide
Hymns of luminous seers to adorn
Force upon them riches magnified

So many riches, so much delight
And issues. A paragon offspring, so bright

2.2.12

Who sings for Agni such hymns, such vow
Freedom, the luminous wise must endorse
Agni, a gift steered by the rays of the cow
What form is that, but of the horse

Lead us to a world where riches are many
Where, strength can I gain
Power from the heroes friendly
Let the vast voice to knowledge begin

2.2.13

Bhargava

I present Agni, Jataveda, our guest
I, Brighu serves him best
Deity among deities; in waters crest
Set him old in our house at rest

At Brighu's behest
Agni is Sovran, god's envoy blessed

2.4.1-2.4.2

Within human tribes in their rite
Agni sent by the gods to the finite
A dear friend shines in a longing night
In his sweet growth we find delight

As he rushes to burn despite
Darting his tongue, shaking his tail bright

2.4.3-2.4.4

Some honor me, praise me great
He gave a hue to those who love him
Known is he, from his bright, charming state
The waxing old turns to trim and slim

2.4.5

Thirsty, he burns the woods riding a car that roars
A dark path he blazes, beauty he pours
Marked in the heavens are his thirst shores
Smiles loom through the crimson vapors

2.4.6

Traversing the earth, an ox, no herdsman
Burnt bushes, blackened lines mark his span
Third is a meet, a song in tribute to a plan
Agni's offer of wealth, an offspring in our clan

2.4.7-2.4.8

Gritsamada serves in secret
Agni, he's the neighbor's covet
Riches, heroes, subdued foes frequent
The vital power given to singers great

2.4.9

The herald took birth as a teacher
And a guardian to patrons' service
Earned is he from rites by this preacher
Strong he is, may we grasp his purpose

2.5.1

Seven reins set for this sacrificial leader
Who advances human-like to an eighth
Swift, bird-like he chants the holy prayer
Knowledge in grasp, felly turns a wheel of faith

2.5.2-2.5.3

Pure is his mental power, pure he directs
True to his laws, he waxes like an old limb
Clothed in his hues, on him the leader awaits
Better than the three are the sisters in prim

2.5.4-2.5.5

Sister by a Mother, laden with a holy oil
Priest relishes corn when comes the rain
In support, he plays his priestly roil
A song of praise, can we obtain?

2.5.6-2.5.7

This man super skilled
Worships the holy one
And, to Agni, the sacrifice we build
Prepared to be the someone

2.5.8

Agni, will you accept a flaming brand?
Will you listen to my songs of praise?
Seek the horses to hear a hymn so grand
Fair hymn plays your birth in a noble race

2.6.1-2.6.2

Agni, lover of songs indulges in affluence
With reverence is this special worship
Prince reigns the precious with prudence
Abolish our haters, protect us by your grip

2.6.3-2.6.4

Rain from heaven, food in plenty
None other than what you give
Holy herald, hold not to that bounty
Craving help, through our song, relive

2.6.5-2.6.6

You switch between Agni and Sage
Envoy, friend to the human mass
Help us reach the gods in every stage
Take a seat on this sacred grass

2.6.7-2.6.8

Bhargava

Young Vasu, Bharata, Agni, bring us wealth
We desire this excellent bounty
Let nothing alter god's or man's health
Save us from this horrific enmity

2.7.1-2.7.2

Give us power to drive the enemy away
Force the water from a flooded soil
Powerful shine, bright, adorable ray
They worship Agni with sacred oil

2.7.3-2.7.4

Agni, the honor is ours, Bharata among all
Take the barren cows, bullocks and cattle
The ancient, wood-fed, dipped in sacred oil
Son of strength, wonderful is your dazzle

2.7.5-2.7.6

Gritsamada

Agni's ageless car, fair to check upon
Him, they extol night and day at a home
Unbroken laws, shines like the Sun
Decked in an imperishable glossy dome

2.8.1-2.8.4

Atri, Agni, lift our songs today
He owns every glory outright
Agni, Indra, Soma and gods at bay
Unhurt, together, beat those who fight

2.8.5

Settled by a bright herald, fine, n' mighty
Agni's acumen spares the law from violation
Envoy he is, guards us from foes actively
Strong Agni for our progeny expansion

2.9.1-2.9.2

Agni adored at his birthplace
Endorses the best gift to present
Brings the gods to bless us with their grace
Shines with affluence, turns it pleasant

2.9.2-2.9.6

Agni calls aloud, kindled on a worship seat
Magnificent robes, gilded by the famous
Agni, listen to my songs with your insight
Red steeds draw his car, they are gracious

2.10.1-2.10.2

On wood strewn flat sits a well-formed infant
Germinates he, in many a plant and tree
Uncovered in the dark shroud of the night
Rays of splendor, astute he smiles in glee

2.10.3

Agni peppered in gifts and oil
Built a home around all things living
His broad, vast, vital power over all
Strong turns he, with food that feed his being

2.10.4

In every direction he stares, I pour for him
A polite groom, will he accede to a color intact?
Like Manu, we speak, we appreciate his serving
Perfect Agni, his tongue dashes a sweet impact

2.10.5-2.10.6

Visvamitra

Strong Agni makes me Soma's priest
Shines He for gods, I toil with press-stones
To east is the rite, hymns of wood aid the feast
Heaven's clergy seeks to advance the tones

3.1.1-3.1.2

Prudent, with his pure will, he means well
In heaven and earth, joined in birth by kin
In waters' midst, on Agni, the eyes of gods fell
Appeared he, through the sister's labor therein

3.1.3

Add the seven strong floods
White at birth, he waxes red
Mother mare runs to a new-born with hugs
When Agni assumed birth, gods wondered

3.1.4

Radiant limbs engulf every region, n' quarter
Purged, his powers harbor an astute challenge
Robed in light, he lives a life on water
High in glory he rides the aqueous range

3.1.5

In heaven, he sought the undevoured perfect
What appeared unclothed and yet not nude
Ancient, yet young; he dwelt as a single object
And seven rivers merged to honor him good

3.1.6

Assuming every form, he emerged in a scatter
Where flow sweet waters in bulky spring
A stoic, milky rays of a full-laden udder
Pairs of mothers rush to the amazing thing

3.1.7

Carefully cherished, a blazing son of strength
Shines he in a beauty undying and bright
Descends streams of fat, sweet juice at length
At once, he grows strong in the wisdom's light

3.1.8

At birth, he glimpsed his father's heart
He knows who stirs with friends in secret
With young dames in heaven, nothing covert
He lets his voice stream to a motion perfect

3.1.9

He tends to the infant of the sire, the maker
The babe suckles many a crowded breast
To the bright and strong, he is a protector
In his kinship, how did spouses invest?

3.1.10

The One grows in valor in the etheric space
To Agni, a glorious offering steeped in force
In order's lap lolls Agni, house friend in place
Busy in the service of a sister's river course

3.1.11

Bracing a region where the great waters meet
He, a light-shedder is a joy to look upon
When things go awry, he's there to beget
Youthful Agni, is man the light of dawn?

3.1.12

Infant in a flood, woods reckon his gender
Gods in spirit serve him at his birth
Lightnings usher Agni, light spread by a runner
Waxes in secret, milks Amrita in a hearth

3.1.13-3.1.14

In this sacrifice, I crave Agni's goodwill and bond
With the gods, grant us every defensive ray
Agni leads fair, mastering treasures beyond
Noble child in battle placates the godless away

3.1.15-3.1.16

Emblem of the gods you are
Agni, you know every secret wisdom
You travel to the gods in your car
A farm faded friend marks your kingdom

3.1.17

Immortal king in the houses of few
Agni soaked in holy oil, shines far n' wide
Come quick with aid when we ask of you
Grant us wealth, let our repute be our pride

3.1.18-3.1.19

To ancient Agni, modern yet old songs
Every birth the Jataveda can unveil
Birth kindled by clan where Visvamitra belongs
In the holy love, respite we shall avail

3.1.20-3.1.21

This sacrifice to gods who will rejoice
Agni, award us food and wealth when you can
As food, furnish us a cattle of choice
Be born a son to spread the clan

3.1.22-3.1.23

Visvamitra Gathinah

The holy law, Vaisvanara braces to adhere
Pure Agni, our praise of oil at the altar
Our thoughts, an insight to bring him near
Herald of the old. An axe forms your car

3.2.1

His birth dazzles heaven and earth's honor
After birth, two mothers appeal for him
Agni, gracious n' young, endures the offer
To our guest in radiant light, our hymn

3.2.2

The immense powers of the gods feed
They create Agni in their inventive thought
Eager for strength, I address him like a steed
Burning brilliant with ample light to allot

3.2.3

Hopes of gaining strength and Brighu's gift
Inspired by the sages' customs, lit in heaven
A trimmed sacred grass beckons Agni's seat
Ladles raised to Agni; Rudra rites turn solemn

3.2.4-3.2.5

At the priest's home, men trim the sacred grass
As a service for Agni to grant them wealth
Will heaven and earth in his light engross?
Is he a sacrificial horse led by a Sage in stealth?

3.2.6-3.2.7

Yes, honor the divine high priest's stance
Oblige the wise friend's occupation
He, who drives a chariot of lofty ordinance
Highly active Agni bears the oblation

3.2.8

Envious of Agni, who defies death to come
Pure, his three splendors, he circles there
For human enjoyment, he lends one
Spread are other two in his sister's sphere

3.2.9

Sacrificial food sharpened with an axe
For his brightness, the sage and lord
In sacred rites, his up-down moves never go lax
He germinates in the worlds by accord

3.2.10

Stirs in life in wombs not similar
Born a lion, a bellowing bull
Immortal Vaisvanara with a wide sliver
Bestows wealth and gifts in full

3.2.11

Ancient Vaisvanara mounts the heaven's ridge
Greeted by folks who sing him a noble song
As in past, the folks, he makes them rich
Watchful, in the common he traverses along

3.2.12

Agni we seek, for a new prosperity
Maatarisvan initiates him in heaven
To meet high praise and the holy
Sage, true to the law, offers no pretend

3.2.13

Pure and swift, the light it spawns
We spot in heaven's bright sphere a sign
Agni, head of heaven wakes to the dawns
Will I access power from this prayer's design?

3.2.14

Cheerful, the priest, with no deceit
Household friend, dear to humankind
Behold his splendid car, so fair to greet
Agni, in you, we seek wealth, human friend

3.2.15

Visvamitra Gathinah

See Vaisvanara sparkle at a distance
Valued gifts from a bard on a trail
Immortal Agni, to the deities he grants
Series of everlasting laws not known to fail

3.3.1

Gods sent Agni enriched with prayer
Now he travels between earth and heaven
With rays he visits a tall launch layer
Seated as the herald, high priest of men

3.3.2

Sages sing Agni's glory in earnest
Banner of sacrifice fills the clergy
Singers stock holy acts at his behest
Devotees seek joy in this journey

3.3.3

Chief of sacrifice, leader of holy bards
Iconic Agni, the priests measure him with
Visits to heaven and earth he sets records
The sage's love rejoices in his myth

3.3.4

In greens n' floods, Vaisvanara spots the light
Bright Agni swift in a vivid car
Pervasive, nimble, wild in the powers of bright
Glorious Agni establishes the gods in far

3.3.5

Agni, gods n' Manu's folks in sight
Extend the thought sacrifice, make it vary
In a car, they go around crowning each rite
House friend reverses every curse not ordinary

3.3.6

Sing for a long life, sons of noble
Pour in plenty, shine on us the food
Grow the great man's strength to double
Longing for gods, sing them hymns of good

3.3.7

Mighty lord of people, leader of thought
Jataveda, friend of priests, men ever praise
Stunning Agni, from joy, deprive us not
On his lovely car, the lands you traverse

3.3.8-3.3.9

I acclaim Vaisvanara's glory in the end
The farsighted deity locates the light
Agni, the light at birth fills earth and heaven
Has he gone around himself tonight?

3.3.10

Skilled sage passes a great deed
Grander than Vaisvanara's acts indeed
Agni springs into being to his parents need
Rich, heaven n' earth bloom with a prolific seed

3.3.11

Visvamitra Gathinah

Against the dawn, he wakes to shine
Holy singer precedes the sage's kindness
Ranges far, his luster, kindled in time
Priest throws open the gates of darkness

3.5.1

Agni pales in might when they pour the laud
Softened by hymns when they stop to praise
In the show of holy order when bowed
Agni shines at the first flush of a dawn phase

3.5.2

Within homes, Agni resides
Friend fulfills the law, a seed from water
Sages love the heights he ascends
To the Singer, our invocations matter

3.5.3

Agni turns Mitra when enkindled
Mitra becomes Varuna, Jataveda-s, priest
Mitra then, as active minister and house-friend
Mitra of rivers and mountains in east

3.5.4

Earth's, 'n the Bird's place he sets to guard
Protects by his might, Surya's course at par
Guards he, a Seven-headed, undeterred
Guards the deities' inspiring instant in no fear

3.5.5

The skilled god who knows all therein
Built for himself, a fair skin ready for revere
Agni guards with care the durable Soma skin
The Bird's place rich in layers of fat austere

3.5.6

Agni enters a desirous shrine, layered in fat
Giving easy access to every other
Fiery, pure, the sublime aristocrat
Repeatedly, he renovates his twin Mother

3.5.7

Sudden his birth, he grows within an herb
Tender shoots in holy oil make him bigger
Like fallen waters as they cascade n' perturb
Agni in parents' lap, may he protect forever

3.5.8

Praised, a strong one gleams, kindled with fuel
From earth's center, rises he to heaven's height
Friend Agni, sweet Maatarisvan, a plea crucial
As envoy, please bring the gods to prayer tonight

3.5.9

Agni's flame keeps safe the heights of heaven
Far from Brighu, Maatarisvan kindles the devotee
For an aspirant, wealth in cattle does Agni beckon
Born as son, his will's grace does he oversee

3.5.10-3.5.11

Visvamitra Gathinah

Deep devotion sets the urge
Singers, set the moral, bring the divine ladle
Set to the right, for Agni in east, let it diverge
Filled to the brim with the oil fuel

3.6.1

At birth, you filled earth, heaven went past
Beyond heaven, rolled a seven-tongued fiery cluster
Heaven, earth and gods set you as priest at first
Mortals and gods laud your splendid luster

3.6.2-3.6.3

Firm sits the mighty in a paradise of home
Unhurt rays yield nectar, unite the divine spouse
Great, power in earth and heaven to roam
He took birth, an envoy thereabouts

3.6.4-3.6.5

Holy cords bind the ruddy horse to a pole
Sprinkling fat, Jataveda; a divine prayer we offer
Light from sky beamed by the morning patrol
Gods smile; a forest burnt by Agni's ardor

3.6.6-3.6.7

Gods enjoy Vayu's expanse of wide
Divine dwellers euphoric on the sight of bright
Even the holy, they prompt to hear the side
Who in their cars turn their steers right

3.6.8

Place on one ear, Agni, start your approach
Place on different ears, your horses manage
Bring every goddess, their god in that coach
Thirty-three in your divine, joy's passage

3.6.9

Restore order, sing, priest of heaven n' earth
In holy food, give wealth through cattle
Come forward to them in a sacrifice's worth
Agni assures a son's birth to our dazzle

3.6.10-3.6.11

Visvamitra Gathinah

Seven tones from a dish with rice plain
Make their way to mothers in two
Surrounding parents prepare to hasten
Length of days they yield for you

3.7.1

Male in heaven owns a mare and cow
He offers each goddess a sweet treasure
Rest safe in the seat of order though
Cow walks the path of her rays as before

3.7.2

Rich master climbs to the seeker to help
Dark-backed, brush-wood springs from a meal
Streams tow him forever, Tvastar's job upkept
Burning domestic, reduce two worlds to one

3.7.3-3.7.4

Red bull blesses flame's dominion in delight
Ila honors those who sparkle from heaven
Singer's bull ousted at night, his law takes flight
Sages by tradition fetch strength of the Parent

3.7.5-3.7.6

Seven poets, five Adhvaryu picket the Bird's post
Bulls who don't age, gods rejoice in them
Heaven's two thrill in seven steeds they mount
Truth praised eternal, guards the order of flame

3.7.7-3.8.8

Great stallion, many seek, many laud
Reins obey the lord in a color festoon
You, priest of heaven, bring for us every god
Bring to earth and heaven their boon

3.8.9

Rich, fiery lord in mornings gleam forth
Fair his rays, fair his speech he will transmit
Agni, to you is this glory of earth
Forgive us for the sin we commit

3.8.10

Agni, give a devotee wealth of cattle as food
Lasting wealth, rich in the marvels of the deep
Let a son be born to us in times good
As the offspring spread, your grace we seek

3.8.11

Agni, how you rule humankind in firm
But mortal man, does he grasp the spark?
They sing to your grace rites so solemn
Laws warden, Agni, shines in the dark

3.10.1-3.10.2

More fuel honors him, he knows all about life
With powers of a hero in him, can he prosper?
Sacrifice banner winched for the gods to arrive
Seven priests adorn who has gifts to offer

3.10.3-3.10.4

Agni, offer your best in a lofty speech
Bring a light, all your songs to match
In hymns you grow, in life's outreach
What a fearsome strength for us to watch

3.10.5-3.10.6

Agni, fetch the gods for pious men
Joyous priest, keeps the foes at arm's length
Kindled in verses of hymns, awaken
Bear the oblation, cherish the strength

3.10.7-3.10.9

Priest Agni, swiftly reconvene
He knows the rite, its constant course
Bear the oblation, messenger so keen
Agni with a thought, will you approach?

3.11.1-3.11.2

Ancient icon his thoughts prepare
Knows man's aim and hope to prosper
Knows about life, eminent from yesteryear
Gods make their priest stronger

3.11.3-3.11.4

Failsafe Agni, he heads the tribe of men
Rides a chariot swift and ever new
He subdues foes time and again
No fame comes close to Agni's avenue

3.11.5-3.11.6

With sacred food, bathes a home in light
Our hymns, will they bring wealth and joy
Singers know he knows all life despite
The gods centered around Agni boy

3.11.7-3.11.9

Indra-Agni arrive by hymns, sip the nectar
Sip the juice, impelled by this song
They realize the wakening rite in a prayer
For both assured is this drink strong

3.12.1-3.12.2

Wise reckon Indra-Agni, a sacrificial force
Soma satiates them here
Joint victors Indra and Agni I endorse
Unsubdued bounteous foe-slayer they are

3.12.3-3.12.4

Hymn for Indra and Agni, singers compose
I elect them to a taste of the sacred food
Ninety forts of Dasa-s[40], they destroy, dispose
Together, in one mighty act of good

3.12.5-3.12.6

Our reverence for them; what a holy task?
They cruise the path of sacred law
Dwelling, food, power from them we ask
Such act of good n' strength, sing with awe

3.12.7-3.12.9

Rishabha Vaisvamitra

I sing aloud to Agni with much power
To arrive with gods, sit on the grass again
Earth and heaven are his, help wanted this hour
In his grace, we hope to gain

3.13.1-3.13.2

Leader of sacred rites, he guides men
May Agni grant shelter in his shine
He pours wealth in floods 'n heaven
Kindled, no peer, by his own design

3.13.3-3.13.5

Bramha[41], in this hymn, please bless
In the Marut team, beam on us the bliss
Grant wealth, children, thousands, no less
Exalted Agni, please don't dismiss

3.13.6-3.13.7

---

[40] As we get closer to the Vishnu transition, Vishnu (younger sibling) helps Indra in vanquishing Vritra and destroying ninety-nine fort-cities of RV 7.99.5

[41] Ut nau Bramhannavish – Later texts reckon Bramha as the divine cause for making the creatures. Agni assumes the role of the maker.

In the clergy, a pleasant, skilled priest
Son of strength, hair enflamed in blister
His car, a lightning at its least
On earth, he displays his luster

3.14.1

I offer a humble speech; accept it
To the known, please convey
Those who know will commit
Come sit on the grass thatch today

3.14.2

Night and morning show their vigor
Use the wind's path, they hasten to you
Men garnish the Ancient with their prayer
They seek an asylum on chariot-seats of two

3.14.3

Song from Varuna, Mitra, Marut team
They sing a song of triumph to brighten
When into the people's land will you stream?
Spread the luster of the Sun of men

3.14.4

With raised hands, with respect, we approach
We fulfill this day in your longing
Prayer for every god, learned from a coach
Aided by a friendly priest affirming

3.14.5

Son of strength has many a relief
Powers so abundant only a god can possess
Grant us wealth, true speech n' belief
Make them real, in thousands afresh

3.14.6

The god molded in sacrifice by mortal man
It is for you, strong, wise in purpose
Be friend to every good charioteer band
Immortal Agni, enjoy what you chose

3.14.7

Utkila Katya

Stunning in an array of luster
Dispel the beasts' terror that live in hatred
Agni, be my guide and shelter
Easily invoked, protector sacred

3.15.1

Step in for us; the morning breaks through
Be a guardian when the sun climbs high
Accept my laud, like you would, an infant new
Your birth in a body, noble does it qualify

3.15.2

Bull, men honor in the morning
Among the dark flames, shine in red
Lead, stop the plights before they begin
Help them seek the rich knowhow instead

3.15.3

Shine, bull invincible, shine
Overthrow every fort and treasure
Jataveda-s, skilled in guiding
Chief is he, the sacrifice's forerunner

3.15.4

Agni, the lighting deities arrive, wise singer
Fetch us a flawless shelter
Bring the car's vigor that gathers treasure
Bring the exquisite earth n' heaven together

3.15.5

Bull, expand to access powers on urge
Earth and heaven yield their rays in plenty
Shine with the deities in a fiery charge
Don't let a mortal's evil mind obstruct any

3.15.6

Agni, give the holy food to your invoker
Give wealth from cattle, rich in every wonder
Sons when born, let our clan swagger
Agni, your grace grows in grandeur

3.15.7

Agni reigns pleasure and strength
Lord of cattle wealth battles the foe
Marut-s, please wait, prosperity is wealth
To the evil-hearts in a fight, he deals a blow

3.16.1-3.16.2

Agni, allocate the wealth, the hero's might
Let the progeny go disease free to power
Redefine life, order services to a god's delight
Works among gods with strength to shower

3.16.3-3.16.4

No penury, give us the hero son
No lack of cattle, drive the enemy away
Strengthen the sacrifice in turn
Flood us with riches, plenty to play

3.16.5-3.16.6

Kata Vaisvamitra

Kindled with old customs, embalmed is he
Flame-haired, bring the gods to worship
Jataveda, priest of earth n' heaven, the almighty
In Manu's offering, hope the gods show up

3.17.1-3.17.2

Jataveda, three lifetimes, three mornings of birth
With them grant Lord's favor to a worshipper
Jataveda Agni, fair, bright, our song's worth
Gods make you center of life's eternal power

3.17.3-3.17.4

The priest before you, skilled more in worship
Established in the past, health-giver his nature
Lay our sacrifice where gods taste it's drip
You know best his custom offer

3.17.5

Kind Agni, lets advance, friend to a friend
Let's befriend you as a sire and mother
Every race of man oppresses with pretend
Burn the malice, let struggle none other

3.18.1

Agni, burn the hostile next to our group
Scorch the ruffian's spell, who wages no worship
Vasu burn, you mark those who dupe
Eternal light-beams encircle your lordship

3.18.2

Agni first in fuel, then in oil, my offering
In return, give me strength in the conquest?
I sing the power prayer, speak adoring
Warm hymns gain hundreds of asset

3.18.3

Son of strength in a glow unfurl
Promise a great critical influence
Riches for Visvamitra caught in rest and swirl
Wreathes for your body take a chance

3.18.4

Will a liberal lord pour riches and tell?
Agni, generous you are, when we kindle you
Promise the happy singer where to dwell
With arms extended, give a thing of beauty too

3.18.5

Gathinah Kaushik

Unfailing Agni, sagacious, all-knowing
Reckon, I am the priest at this oblation
Services to the god ongoing
Bring strength, and riches with no negation

3.19.1

Agni, I lift the bright, oil-fed ladle
I promise an offering, stamped in oblation
Gods' turnout using the right hand enabled
With riches he presents a worship in session

3.19.2

Profound turns his spirit with Agni's help
Freely you give the boon of a good offspring
Fancy riches likened to power of wealth
Praises for your nobility let me sing

3.19.3

Only you, they adore and no one
Agni, a brilliant aspect on you they offer
Bring the gods' assembly, young one
Heavenly host today for your honor

3.19.4

Gods anoint you priest in men's prayer
Seat assigned for you in the sacrificial duty
Agni, become then our kind defender
Vouchsafe the gift of glory

3.19.5

Break of morn, a priest turns to invoke
Agni, Usha, Dadhikra[42] and the Ashvin two
Will god hear? His light a splendid stroke
He longs to taste our sacrifice; will he hear too?

3.20.1

---

[42] Dadhikra is a divine horse or bird, personifies the Sun

Powers of three, in stations three, Agni'll begin
Tongues there are three; many, therein
Body of three, which the gods delight in
With every three, protect our hymns unceasing

3.20.2

Agni, many names you bear
Jataveda, immortal, god, divine, few on record
Many charms of a charmer you may spare
Lured in you, a true attendants lord

3.20.3

Agni, as Bhaga, leads the divine men
True to the law, he has seasons to guard
Ancient Agni, the Vritra slayer time again
Spares the singer from any distress afterward

3.20.4

It's morning, I call on Savitr, the sun god
Brihaspati, Dadhikra, Agni, I pray
Varuna, Mitra, the Ashvin team I applaud
N' Bhaga, Vasu, Rudra and Aditya portray

3.20.5

Reset the sacrifice among the immortal few
Jataveda, do the presents entice you?
Priest Agni, sit with us, your devoted crew
Enjoy first drops of oil, then a fatty residue

3.21.1

For him, flow drops of fat, smeared in oil
Grant us a boon, gods may feast
Agni, drops of sages drip from oil
Kindled as a seer, help the sacrifice, O priest

3.21.2-3.21.3

Agni, none dare defy your power
Fuel stream moves with drops of oil and fat
You arrive with great light at this hour
Accept this offering of praises from a poet

3.21.4

Fat, cut from middle better than our gift
Agni, excellent as a god, I feel awed
Fiery beads pour down your skin in swift
Present the drippings to every god

3.21.5

It's Agni, Indra feels it embroil
Deep pressed Soma, his body on blaze
Swift as horses in thousands, wining the spoil
Jataveda, exalts you nothing short of praise

3.22.1

Agni, in plants, in deep water
His light in earth and heaven
Where he spreads wide in mid quarter
Bright splendor, wavy, beheld by men

3.22.2

Agni, to the sea of heaven will travel
Summons the gods here in spirit
Waters, too, comes here to unravel
Water up in Sun's light, water beneath it

3.22.3

Fire in the floods, fire in the mist
The candid accepts sacrifice of great food
Agni humors food, where cattle-wealth persist
Be born to us an offspring accrued

3.22.4

Visvamitra Gathinah

Rubbed into life, established well
Leader of sacrifice, young sage
Jataveda, eternal in the wasting fuel
Assumes the immortal, undying age

3.23.1

Bharata, Devasrava, Devavata[43] rub you strong
To life they beckon, capable you become
Expect you to fetch riches all along
Every day to bear food and feed some

3.23.2

Fingers counted ten produced him, born of old
His Mothers counted to have him onboard
Agni of *Devavata*, our praises for him in bold
Devasrava is he; he must be people's lord

3.23.3

Placed is he in earth's charming station
That's Ila's place, when days are bright
Shine, Agni on *Apaya*[44], and on man
On *Drisadvati*[45], on *Sarasvati*, shine your light

3.23.4

Agni indulges in food, where cattle-wealth persist
Will they last? Will they be rich in marvels?
His birth as an offspring, we insist
His grace on us, we seek it's sparkle

3.23.5

Agni, will you subdue these opposing mobs?
Unbeatable, will you drive enemies away?
Eliminate godless foes before they do their jobs
Offer splendor to a worshipper's way

3.24.1

Agni, lit with libation, calls the gods to feast
Accepts our sacrifice with joy
Agni, son of strength with splendor released
Sits on the sacred grass, our worship to enjoy

3.34.2-3.24.3

---

[43] Members of the Visvamitra clan
[44] Apaya is a negative place in the Vedic context.
[45] Drisadvati - The Drisadvati river is the route of the Vedic river
Sarasvati and the state of Brahmavarta.

Offer your grace with your fire
With the gods, bless the songs we've sung
Bless the holy rites, their living sire
Grant in plenty, make us rich with many a son

3.24.4-3.24.5

Wise son of Dyau[46], a child of earth
Expert, bring the gods to our prayer
Wise Agni, in a hero's might let there be no dearth
Will you grant wholesome food, prep it with nectar

3.25.1-3.25.2

Agni, while unfailing you are
Earth and Heaven, you light
Goddesses flash their grace from far
From force to a lord, super in values right

3.25.3

Agni and Indra arrive at a sacrifice
Arrive with gods, where Soma is plenty
Flooded habitats, Jataveda, kindle nice
Bless the gathering-places, you do gently

3.25.4-3.25.5

Revered Agni Vaisvanara, you found light
Promises you keep true, a car borne god
Kusika's oblation to you, liberal is the rite
Seeking wealth with song is the Kusika[47] laud

3.26.1

Agni, Vaisvanara bright, we invoke for relief
Is Maatarisvan worthy of the song of praise?
Brihaspati, an observance of gods, we believe
Singer listens prompt, guest's move in grace

3.26.2

---

[46] Dyau - sky, space.
[47] Kusika – a blade of grass.

In every age, Vaisvanara, the horse, he neighs
Kindled is he by Kusika with women silent
Agni wakes among immortal gods, he weighs
Grant the strength and wealth in steeds so gallant

3.26.3

Blaze of might, go strong, go forth
For victory, the spotted deer is on the yoke
Flood generators, Marut, master of wealth and worth
Unconquered they walk, 'n mountains choke

3.26.4

Marut team, human friend, glorious as fire
Mighty, resplendent succor we implore
Storm raising sons of Rudra, in rain attire
O' the boons they give, their leonine roar

3.26.5

Band of troops pray on Agni's wealth portion
Fair our lauds; they match Marut's might
Spotted deer replaces steed, unfailing the fortune
Wise is One, to come to our sacrifice site

3.26.6

Agni am I, who knows every creature's birth
My eye is butter, my mouth nectar
I, light threefold, limitless my heat on earth
Burnt is every oblation, I alone am its vector

3.26.7

Bear in mind, a thought with light
Purified he, the Sun with refines of three
He gained insight, high treasure outright
Beyond earth and heaven to see

3.26.8

When flow hundred brooks, spring stops not
Father inspired prayer; men try utter
Sparks of joy, in his Parents' heart
Fills earth and heaven with no clutter

3.26.9

Ladle drips oil, oblation food rises to heaven
Travels to the gods in search of bliss
Agni, sage inspired, with this song I beckon
Please listen, fill us with bounteous gifts

3.27.1-3.27.2

Agni, can we attain your control?
Potent lord, can we overcome every foe?
Lit at a sacrifice, revered in a stronghold
Enflamed hair, we seek him though

3.27.3-3.27.4

Immortal Agni, far spreads his shine
Robed in oil, he bears the sacrificial gift
Priests hold ladles, holy thoughts align
They bring Agni to our aid swift

3.27.5-3.27.6

With wondrous powers to usher
This great assembly does he shepherd
Strong, deeds of strength, his buffer
The Singer completes the rite undeterred

3.27.7-3.27.8

Invented by thought, germ of beings to gain
Which all die, you know O' sire of strength
I strengthen you in sage's prayer with no pain
I long for you Agni, you are nobly adept

3.27.9-3.27.10

Singers, sing to the active one
They kindle all food to fire
Agni, shines in heaven solemn
The wise at heart, I desire

3.27.11-3.27.12

A meeting of lauds, beauty in the dark
Agni, the strong, kindled as a bull
Men with oblations with no remark
We as bulls, O Bull, shine in full

3.27.13-3.27.15

Agni, accept our offering and cake
Usha's libation, enriched by the prayer
Agni, we prepared, dressed the cake to bake
Youthful god, you will like its flavor

3.28.1-3.28.2

Agni, enjoy the cake, three days of prayer
Jataveda, at midday enjoy the cake's array
Enjoy the cake at the third offer
Waxing Agni, accept the cake of yesterday

3.28.3-3.28.6

Friction gear, n' brushwood ready for the flicker
Bring the wife, rub Agni to discover
Within the two firesticks, is the Jataveda pillar
Well-set germ as in an expectant mother

Agni exalted by man and his brother
They watch with a prayer to offer

3.29-1-3.29.2

Lay with care on what lies stretched
Straight she bears the Steer when prolific
His red pillar, his colors radiantly etched
Born, son of Ila, in a skilled task so mystic

3.29.3

In Ila's place is he set down
Unto the center of earth with many a laud
Agni Jataveda in his fiery crown
Bear our offerings to every god

3.29.4

Sages and the naive rub you into life
Agni's sacrificial banner faces east
Rubbed into life, red in color, let him strife
Free on Ashvin's path burns the grass beneath

3.29.5-3.29.6

Agni, a singer, wins the sages praise
Gods position him at the rites to bear offers
Men, set the sacrifice at a home these days
Assures a long life, who works with honors

3.29.7-3.29.8

Friends raise a big smoke to win wealth
Agni, gods overpower Dasyu through you
In this ordered place, to life you shine forth
All-knowing, sit down to our songs, review

3.29.9-3.29.10

Tanunapat, he is a celestial gem of wonder
Narasamsa he is born in a diffused shape
As *Maatarisvan*, he is a fetus in his mother
He, rapid flight of wind over a landscape

3.29.11

Abrasive, rubbed to life, by a vigilant sage
Agni jolts the sacrifice to move gods to front
Mortals make a mighty jaws of age
Ten unwed sisters grasp a new-born infant

3.29.12-3.29.13

Seven priests serve his gleams from ancient time
In Mother's bosom, her lap, he glows prime
Every day's a delight, eyes close in time
From Asura's dread, life with no crime

3.29.14

Even as Marut twins attack the foe
Born first, they know the power of prayer
Kusika team raise the hymn to glow
Each in his home kindle the powerful fire

3.29.15

O priest, we elect you this day
Not caring when solemn sacrifices begin
You worship 'n toil every way
Unto Soma, you know the wise therein

3.29.16

101

Vamadeva Gautama

With god's consent Agni comes to earth
Select messenger, god's worth
Immortal for mortal, the god's bring forth
Brought the ever-present sage's birth

4.1.1

Agni fetches Varuna his brother
They love the sacrifice, true to the law
An Aditya, he cares for men who gather
Supports human as royalty who have no flaw

4.1.2

Will you friend, turn our friend here
Swift as a wheel, two rapid car-steeds
Wonderful to watch them appear
Agni, find grace in Varuna for our needs

Find grace in Marut team who illumine all
Bless our progeny, yea lord, bless us all

4.1.3

Don't you Agni know Varuna well?
Keep down his wrath let it not swell
Bright fire, best priest I can tell
No room for haters in this secure shell

4.1.4

Comfort us, Agni, stay near
Closest ally at the break of Morn
Reconcile Varuna, be swift to hear
Give wealth; take the nectar you yearn

4.1.5

Excellent is his glance, it's brilliant
What a propitious deity confers on every mortal
His glance, we wish to attract this instant
Pure butter heated high, it's sparkle

4.1.6

Three reasons for Agni's birth
That, he is true, exalted and longed for
Agni, to any region, there's no dearth
Radiant, friendly, mighty and pure

4.1.7

Envoy's joy in every seat of worship
Cruising a gold car, his sweet tongue invokes
Gorgeous red steeds on this trip
Sumptuous feasts - his many cloaks

4.1.8

In prayer, knowledge he gives man
Extended cord leads him onward
In a mortal's dwelling is his span
God wins a share in his reward

4.1.9

We let him thrive in good health
What the immortal prepares with his wisdom
What he enjoys of a god-sent wealth
True blessings of *Dyau*, *Bhaga* raining down

4.1.10

At home in heaven's base, regions chest
He springs into life for sure
No foot, no head, his ends pressed
His bull's lair holds him secure

4.1.11

He rises in a Bull's lair
Reaches a place of holy order
Young, beautiful, with seven other
He turns larger

He fulfils the sacred law
Human fathers often blunder
Force into Usha's packed bid in a cavern
Know they will not charge further

4.1.12-4.1.13

Splendid, they rent the mountain
Others speak of their exploit
This song they sing, free the cattle again
The light they find, hymns holy adroit

4.1.14

Eager, intent on the treasure
Celestial speech unboxes the supine
Mountain solid, firm, compact it's enclosure
Stable full of cattle, stray cows they confine

4.1.15

Cow's earliest name to comprehend
To find Mother's thrice-seven noble title
This, the bands knew, they acclaimed
In the Bull's sheen, red One ostensible

4.1.16

Dark chaos flees, striking opens the heaven
Up rises a bright beam in a morning celestial
Surya ascends the wide expanse to beckon
He watches every deed of good and evil

4.1.17

When they look around awake
They stare at the divine treasure
Every god seated in their homes by daybreak
Varuna, Mitra effective with their prayer

4.1.18

Can I summon Agni beaming bright?
Herald he is, supports everything by prayer
He brings the purest milk of Soma delight
Cleansed, poured from many a beaker

4.1.19

Free to worship is the savior
Guest in our homes, he's so precious
Agni wins every gods favor
May Jataveda be gracious

4.1.20

Agni, immortal amidst every mortal
Deity among every other divine being
A herald, a priest, shines in a glorious circle
Agni held high with man's offering

4.2.1

Your birth again today, son of vigor
Agni, you feature not with any mortal race
You fare well as an envoy figure
Muscled radiant stallion, strong your harness

4.2.2

Ruddy steeds pour blessings, I laud
Oil drips, flicks past your order lit with grace
Red horses yoked, you travel back and forth
Between deities and every mortal race

4.2.3

Aryaman, Mitra, Varuna, Indra, Vishnu gods
Many a Marut and Ashvin brother
Bring them in a sturdy car against the odds
Bring them to folks who brand a fair prayer

4.2.4

Consider Agni, this is our sacrifice eternal
We take part with friends so brave
Agni Asura, cattle, n' horses gathered as normal
Food, children, wealth at your enclave

4.2.5

Perspiring, the man brings you fuel
Aches his head, the servant you trust
Agni, be a part of his defense
From troublemakers, guard him robust

4.2.6

Agni, the man brings you food
Shortages you have none
Welcome a guest with cheerful attitude
Onwards on the run

At home the devout kindles you fulfilled
Secure the wealth n' charity he has build

4.2.7

He sings praises in the morning and night
With oblation he does to your delight
He courses gold-grits at home tonight
Salvage him from grief with treasured light

4.2.8

With uplifted ladle he does his service
Immortal Agni gets many a gift
To save his surplus, his toil he can furnish
No sinner may encircle him in a wicked circuit

4.2.9

Agni, his well-bent prayer to accept
O liberal giver, as god, here's a mortal's gift
His sacrifice, can he even perfect?
Strengthen him when he adores you swift

4.2.10

When he groups sense and folly as separate
Like horses' back, crooked and straight
Agni directs us to offspring and wealth
Penury he sets aside, plenty he gives instead

4.2.11

Such a sage and other sages don't deceive
He is down at a corporeal home
Would a god in rapid perceive?
Behold the fair deities to look upon

4.2.12

Agni, please guide that priest well
For the young god, Soma we outpour
While his ruling men and joyous god dispel
He promises bounty from fruits of labor

4.2.13

Our body and limbs to act
Our faith, strong, convincing
Guided by the rite, the wise toil and act
They ride a car with manual cunning

4.2.14

Mother Usha, the first seven sages urge
Men must learn to enact with strength
Angirasa as sons to heaven converge
In our glow, upset the hill with wealth

4.2.15

The forebears in days bygone
Agni's worship they must've spawn
Seeking pure light, piety; praises they sang
Cleft the ground; appeared red dawn

4.2.16

Gods, in an act of holy, set to install
Smelt the ore for human peers to crawl
Enkindled Agni, exalted Indra above all
Covered the cattle's stall

4.2.17

He marked strong the past gods splendor
In a pasture, like herds feeding
Cattle moan their desire when mortals enter
He'd help the true, nearest living

4.2.18

We worked for you, we labored in might
In worship, bright dawns shed their light
Beauty enhanced Agni, perfect was the sight
God's lovely eye shines eternal bright

4.2.19

Disposer Agni, singing praises we bridge
When you listen, be glad
Blaze high, make us more rich
With your boons, in wealth let us be clad

4.2.20

Rudra, lord of prayer, can we help you?
Two worlds priest, your sacrifice in firm
Agni invests in colors of golden hue
Before the thunder strikes him numb

4.3.1

We made for your visit this shrine
As a fond woman for her man, dresses fine
Perform efficient work, before us sit n' recline
I will invest to meet when the flames incline

4.3.2

Hymns go to the priest in a gentle phase
He looks upon humans with a knowing grace
To the immortal, this song of praise
Soma presser, with elegance he prays

4.3.3

While you know in truth the law
Please stay alert in this solemn rite
When we sing you a festive song
Let peace spread to our home in bright

4.3.4

Agni, to Varuna, to heaven, don't complain
Did we do anything to offend?
To earth, to Mitra, will you speak again?
To Aryaman, Bhaga, don't say in the end

4.3.5

When you blaze on altars of less?
But to tell Vayu, who will always bless
What will you say circling earth's ingress?
To Rudra slaying men, what will you stress?

4.3.6

Don't tell Pusan, he fosters welfare, law-abiding?
Don't tell Rudra, with oblations he is thorough?
Will you squeal sins to Vishnu, the far-striding?
What, Agni, will you tell the Lofty Arrow?

4.3.7

What will you tell the Marut band?
How will you reply Sun when questioned?
Before the free, the swift, will you defend?
Fulfil heaven's work, O Jataveda friend

4.3.8

I beg for cow's true gift of an order forge
Raw, but the sweet ripe juice is her call
Dark is her hue, the milk she'd discharge
Nutritious it is, shining, sustains us all

4.3.9

Agni the Bull, his back, a sparkle
Sprinkled with oil by a law perpetual
Unscathed, he imparts powers of vital
Pure udder offers milk to Prisni, the Bull

4.3.10

By law, Angira's men take the rocks apart
With the cattle, hymns they set forth
Lost in delight, they cover the morn in art
Apparent flows the light at Agni's birth

4.3.11

By law, Apah, immortal goddess
Keep them far, who injure not, intoxicate
Agni cheers a strong steed's progress
Flow in speed, swift; constant his placate

4.3.12

Feast not with neighbors who injure us
Deceitful neighbor, useless kin
Chastise us not for a false trespass
May we feel not a friend or a libel's chagrin

4.3.13

Agni, keep us secure and safe
Warm us in your shelter and love
Drive the foes, destroy the disease
Slay the demon when he convenes above

4.3.14

Songs of praise supplicate your grace
Touch our food, move with our prayer
Angira, accept them, gifts of piety and care
Let the praise of gods address your desire

4.3.15

To dispose, you are known
Wise secret speeches I chant as always
Sung to a sage, these words of wisdom
O Singer, to you, my views and praise

4.3.16

Arrange broad net for a vigorous start
Move as a king does, with his attendant
Pierce the villains with every burning dart
Keep on the swift net, arrows shot constant

4.4.1

On a known flight, let your missiles arraign
Follow them close, watch them glow in fury
Agni, your tongue can spread a winged flame
Unchained, cast around all that's not dreary

4.4.2

Send spies ahead, quick and nimble
Do not remain misled, people's warden
Let him not deceive, near or far, bent on evil
Trouble you send, let it not burden

4.4.3

Agni, rise, give your presence some relief
Burn the foes with arrows that pierce
Agni, blaze on him who portends mischief
Like dried straw devour him fierce

4.4.4

Agni, rise, send them away who wish to fight
Obvious is your own divine vigor
Weaken the bows of the demonic knight
Destroy them, kin or stranger

4.4.5

Young god, with favors to redeem
To a high devotion, he sets the urge
Fair weather days, tons of riches he can beam
Lively on a good man's porch

4.4.6

Favored by Agni, be a generous donor
In his lauds, his oblation, his hymn
Prone to please you with home and honor
Make his days bright, I speak for him

4.4.7

I praise, I sing your amiable favor
My song switches to a lovers tone
Steed and car lord, we decorate your honor
Assure us every day your region, your zone

4.4.8

By free will, let each serve you rich
Brilliant every day, at day and night
May we honor you as we make the switch
Beyond people's glory, in content and delight

4.4.9

His steeds of wonder, attired in fine gold
Arrive, Agni in a richly laden car
His joy lies in entertaining you twofold
In you, he knows his friend, his protector

4.4.10

Power of word and kin, I honor with might
Received from Gautama, my father
Young god, mark our words this night
House friend, wise, he is an invoker

4.4.11

Alert, ever friendly, yet never prone
Sleepless, speedy and propitious
With powers to protect, Agni errs none
Combines their places to preserves us

4.4.12

Agni, your guardian rays cure the righteous
Saves Mamateya from blindness with a service
Lord of riches, he preserves the pious
Foes who harmed before, do no more malice

4.4.13

Your aid, your company brings wealth
Your guidance gives us strength
Fulfil our words, you ever in truth
Turning bolder with power, do this straight

4.4.14

Agni, we have the fuel to serve
We sing a laud for your favor
Destroy the Rakshasas who unnerve
Save us from deceit, scorn and slander

4.4.15

In one accord, how do we give all?
Respects to Agni, Vaisvanara, bounteous, wise
Great light, your uprise is fast and nimble
Just as a pillar bears the roof, support the rise

4.5.1

Censure not this god, self-reliant, civil
Offered his bounty to me, a mortal
Deathless, wise, discerning, so simple
Virile Vaisvanara, Agni youthful

4.5.2

Sharp, piercing, with much vigor
Agni knows the lofty hymn held secret
In the lost cow's track, double power
This buried knowledge will he narrate

4.5.3

With sharp teeth, he floods us rich
Agni, your flame destroys, glowing fierce
Honor Varuna's directives with no glitch
Or don't heed wise Mitra's law of terse

4.5.4

Women with no brothers often stray
Women who hate their men turn disloyal
Immoral, untrue, unfaithful their way
They produce this wicked level

4.5.5

You Agni so luminous; I am weak, innocent
Boldly you give, it is an immense load[48]
The Pristha[49] hymn, profound, dark, diligent
Of seven elements, many delicacies bestowed

4.5.6

Sanctify this song of ours
Using wisdom power, we reach in a twinkling
The Universal One sits on earth's best station
Above Prisni's grassy skin[50] dazzling

4.5.7

Is my discourse complete? Can I say more?
Secret of the milk may I suggest
Someone throws open the cattle stalls door
Bird[51] protects Earths' station loved the best

4.5.8

Just the great one's[52] mighty vision
Which the ancient radiant cow[53] chooses to trail
Shines brightly in the house of order
Swift to the secret, she discovers in detail

4.5.9

---

[48] Guru is the word used. It means heavy in this context
[49] Pristha – special hymn and saman (Gambhir – dark) lost over time. In 5.28.3, "dyuos te pristham rakshatu" indicates protection from Dyau
[50] Prisni means pure, unadulterated. The grass-like skin 'charma' could be a metaphor
[51] Veh – bird. The bird metaphorically means the inner being.
[52] Mahi – the great one.
[53] yad usriya sa chata purvyam gauh – purvyam (past / ancient), usriya (shining, radiant).

Once he glowed fierce with his parent
Recalls he, Prisni's treasure, secret and rational
In the mother cow's lofty station set apparent
A flame bent forward tastes the Bull

4.5.10

With respect Agni, I assert the law's theme
Jataveda, what form must the order happen?
Whatever you are, you are the supreme
Wealth hovers in earth or heaven

4.5.11

Where's wealth and treasure in this tunnel?
Narrate to us Jataveda, you know for sure
What other options in this secret channel?
At a distant place we arrive; there's no censure

4.5.12

Show me the rules threshold and rewards
To contest, a hunting bird speeds as contender
Assemble the goddesses, spouses, their wards
Will Ushas, extend Sun-god's splendor?

4.5.13

Displeased with a speech so weak
Scanty, lacking, and flippant
How dare they address you when they speak!
Who with no weapons, no sorrow evident

4.5.14

Agni, majestic and good in his might
A flame shines in glory where we dwell
Fair he shines, attired in light
Boons cased in wealth, the home shines well

4.5.15

Agni, priest of this rite, stand erect
In gods' service, we sacrifice the best
You rule every thought we set
Wisdom of the pious, you further most

4.6.1

He sets down mid men as priest
To the new clergy, Agni, we beckon
Like Savitr, his splendor runs to a crest
Like a builder, his smoke reaches heaven

4.6.2

Raised is an oil-soaked ladle, glowing fierce
To the right in gods' service seen
Many a circle he turns in reverse
Like a new formed pillar, he ascends keen

Anoints every victim
When he is set firm and trim

4.6.3

Sacred grass strewn; Agni kindled beside
Adhvaryu priest actions exult
Agni tends the cattle right
Goes about three times with a result

4.6.4

Priest Agni, steps in leisure, in fun
Turns, speaking sweet, true to order
Flames run like steed on the run
In fear and awe flee every creature

4.6.5

Beautiful, auspicious is your aspect
Lovely Agni, dreadful when scattering
No splendors shielded in dark effect
On your body, abuse has no ill bearing

4.6.6

His making, no one can hinder
Agni's mother and sire, they freely sent
Companion's benevolence can linger
In human home, where he glows at present

4.6.7

In the habitats of men, they dwelt
Agni, the twice-five sisters created
Roused at day, a spear's tooth bright
Agni's mouth, an axe well-sharpened

4.6.8

Brown steeds drop layers of fat
In vigor, the ruddy speed forward
Great red steed, muscles to look at
To such a service invited are many a god

4.6.9

Agni, bright shining games you play
That move forever, restless, all-subduing
Like falcons that rush to a prey
Bluster aloud like the Marut army moving

4.6.10

To you, flaming god, here is a prayer
Priest's laud, a worship, please give him
Men who establish Agni as invoker
Ready to adore glory of the living

4.6.11

A decree first invoked, came this god's design
Easy to worship, we praise at every rite
Apnavana and Brighu added to his shine
Lit in woods bright to fend homes at night

4.7.1

Agni, your glory we once upheld
Will you come out in the open?
Mortals wish to view the one they held
Adorable in their asylum chosen

4.7.2

On seeing you loyal to the law this way
Sapient and wise, like starry heavens
Lighting the altar with a cheerful ray
At homes, at the solemn rites essence

4.7.3

Vivasvan's emissary of living men
Have chosen their swift emblem
While he rules men time and again
Moving at home like a Brighu flame

4.7.4

Intelligent, he is
They place him as an invoking priest
Sanctifying flame, welcome it is
Witness their might sevenfold increased

4.7.5

Concealed, with no contact
Obscured by eternal mothers in the wood
Though his flames kept secret
Bright turns every side when he thinks good

4.7.6

In earthly udder, as food to spread
Gods rejoice in a home of order
Great Agni, served with respect
Faithful Agni flies to a sacrifice in honor

4.7.7

Birds of each rite, skilled as envoy
Knowing both worlds, what lies in between
From old, you go as willing herald boy
Knowing the secret recess of heaven

4.7.8

Bright deity, your dark path lit by a beacon
Your moving splendor is a wonder at work
When she, a virgin, conceived an icon
Remained an envoy even as a newborn spark

4.7.9

New your birth, your vigor of manhood
Now wind blows on his fiery splendor
His sharp tongue reaches the brushwood
Even solids, his teeth will tender

4.7.10

He suffers food with a swift flame
Strong Agni makes himself a rapid envoy
Tracks the winds rustle, strong his game
He speeds the swift horse onward in joy

4.7.11

Your envoy owns much all along
Immortal, the gift bearer
Woo you with song
I, the best worshipper

4.8.1

With his might he can access
He knows the gift of wealth
Knows the heaven's deep recess
Brings the gods to our earth

4.8.2

He knows as god
How to guide the other god
In his home, the righteous he'll guide
He gives treasures we applaud

4.8.3

An informed herald of worth
A title he can readily earn
He runs his errand back and forth
Knowing the deep recess of heaven

4.8.4

May we gratify him with gifts of sacrifice
Agni, who we kindle to cherish

4.8.5

Famous for wealth, daring their feats
Respect Agni, live in victory and peace

4.8.6

May we receive the bounty everyday
Power and might spring our way

4.8.7

Endowed with strength in high dose
That holy singer sings often
Shoots his arrows swifter than most
Swift channels of the tribes of men

4.8.8

Great are you, great this hum
Agni, some favors will you pass
To this pious man, you have come
Stay seated on the sacred grass

4.9.1

May he the immortal helper
Bard deceived by the pretender
Agni, become his messenger
Become a friend of mortal member

4.9.2

I welcome the chief priest
Around the altar is he led
Invited to this fervent rite
Hotra helps, on a seat is he spread

4.9.3

Agni with fire
At the sacrifice site
In the house as its sire
He, *Bramhan* takes his seat despite

4.9.4

For every kinfolks
Agni is their guide
A sacrifice to celebrate
Men bring oblations fortified

4.9.5

His sacrifice you know well
You serve as his messenger then
Agni's sacrifice will tell
Bear the mortal's gifts to heaven

4.9.6

Be pleased, Angira, pardon this sprawl
Accept our rite, however small
With our sacrifice for all
Give us an ear, listen to our call

4.9.7

In a sacrosanct car
Which you take a ride
You guard those who give by far
Come to us from every side

4.9.8

On this day, we express our care
Agni, Our devoted praise
What you love we bring there
Right judgment, like a horse to a race

4.10.1

You drive a car, judge its speed
Unchecked your strength, Agni of noble
In a lofty sacrifice comes your need
Right judgment stays secretly frugal

4.10.2

Come and meet us, Agni bright
Beckoned by praise and respect
Shine you can, bright as sunlight
Agni, well-disposed in every aspect

4.10.3

May we serve, let the fuel pour
While we chant the laud
Loud as heaven's voice, your blasts roar
On this big day, Agni we applaud

4.10.4

At a time, when there's daylight
At this time of night
You appear sweet and bright
Golden glory, shine within our sight

4.10.5

Spotless, brilliant as gold
Hate and mischief when committed
Gleams the gold on you in bold
Agni, you turn holy to the devoted

4.10.7-4.10.7

Agni, gods with you in honor
Thrive in the friendship of an author
Be our kin, our sponsor
Honor these bonds by the altar

4.10.8

Agni, blessed majesty, a victor
Shine in bright as Surya's neighbor
Splendid you look, even in night's color
Fair looks food in your ardor

4.11.1

Agni, divulge his views, he sings well
He praises you strong in his fervor
Grant him a powerful hymn to excel
Enjoy the hymn with gods you adore

4.11.2

Agni, from you springs poetic wisdom
From you arise hymns that prosper
From you wealth flows, heroes adorn
A true-hearted man offers you a prayer

4.11.3

From you springs a bounty
Helps to bring out the real courage
By gods, you move in bliss gently
Agni, your fleet sets a hasty charge

4.11.4

Agni, your voice sounds pleasant
First among gods to a devout mortal
These hymns we bid to remove the hate
Domicile friend, you are faultlessly cordial

4.11.5

Agni, you detach want and suffering
Every evil you separate
Son of strength, blessed at evening
The good man's welfare, please protect

4.11.6

The man torches you with a raised ladle
To Agni in a day, three meals he offers
Jubilant in your splendor, may he excel
Jataveda turns him wise by mental powers

4.12.1

With labor, he fetches fuel for kindling
Regal Agni's power served in the flow
Agni kindles every evening and morning
He prospers, comes to wealth with no foe

4.12.2

Agni, master of sublime region
Agni, lord of strength and wealth
Now a self-reliant god with reason
Give treasures to a mortal's faith

4.12.3

God in youth, whatever foolish sin
We commit as human
Let Aditi consider us without a sin
Agni, remit our offence, the illusion

4.12.4

Agni, even if it is a great sin
We as friends, save us from hurting
Free us from god's or a mortal's prison
Grant health, strengthen our offspring

4.12.5

You gods, excellent and holy
Release the cow tethered by foot
Free us from this affliction, this folly
Agni, extend our lifespan root

4.12.6

Agni looms, his benevolent mind
On a wealth-giving, radiant, vernal day
Ashvins, come home to a pious kind
Surya, the god, rises in splendor today

4.13.1

Savitr, raises high his luster
A spoil-seeking hero, waves an emblem
Varuna and Mitra join the flutter
Will they let Sun ascend heaven?

4.13.2

They help him push away the dark
Lord of mansions, constant to his object
They behold Sun's universe at work
Seven strong, young horses carry him perfect

4.13.3

Agni spreads a web with a mighty steed
Rends apart the black-hued mantle
Sinking, the Surya rays unsteadily impede
Hides in the dark waters, trickles the gentle

4.13.4

How can he stay unbound, with no support?
He falls not even when directed down
With what self-power does he transport?
He guards the pillar vault of heaven

4.13.5

When Jataveda is ready to meet
Greets Usha striking in her splendor
Agni travels wide in his chariot seat
Nasatyas, come to our sacrifices indoor

4.14.1

Light for every known creature
Savitr raises his banner henceforth
Sunbeams make his presence smoother
Surya fills skies of heaven and earth

4.14.2

Ruddy Usha rides, as fades the last star
Her beams shine hued and mighty
Undeterred, Usha rides her noble car
And, at her approach, men awaken happy

4.14.3

Many a power-driven chariot
Bring the Ashvins at the morning break
More Soma juices flow to the draught
Powered at our sacrifice he'll wake

4.14.4-4.14.5

Agni, the herald of bright
He's but a horse, nimble
Leads us at our solemn rite
God among gods, he is adorable

4.15.1

Three times outright
He shows at a formal rite
Appears Agni, a charioteer, owning a fight
To the gods, he bears food in delight

4.15.2

Agni, wise and merry
Paces the oblations in glee
Lord of strength is he
Priceless boons he gives a devotee

4.15.3

Kindled is he in the east
For Srinjaya, Devavata's son to say the least
Dazzling, he tames the enemy beast

4.15.4

Agni, powerful is his stance
A mortal hero takes a chance
Sharp, his teeth, in which bounties dance

4.15.5

Every day they dress him nigh
A racing horse, they clean and dry
Who will dress the red scion in the sky?

4.15.6

Sahadeva's son with two horses at bay
Thought of me in his sovereign way
Summoned by him I drew not away

4.15.7

Two noble bays he had to offer
I took them without a bother
From Sahadeva's son, not daughter

4.15.8

O Ashvins, may the prince live long
In your care ye gods, we place this son
Son of Sahadeva, Somaka strong

4.15.9

Give more to the youthful prince
The son of Sahadeva to enjoy since
Ashvins, offer him long life, O twins

4.15.10

VISHNU

On Vishnu, the Rig Veda reveals little. Shrouded in mystery, the texts revere the great Vishnu who strode three times to create and navigate the world of three. Three steps lifted him to the highest level, where he resides and upholds the universal law. Some mantra-s on Vishnu and Agni cite their nameless spouses. The scriptures furnish Indra, Soma, Varuna, Agni, Vayu with more features than Vishnu, however the later Brahmanas raise him to a stoic level. Unlike Agni's poignant charisma, Vishnu comes across detached and more aloof. Historians and translators made several attempts to fix the time and meaning of these ancient litanies. Their origin remains a mystery. Fragments in the Brahmanas and Upanishads predict some understanding of the prehistoric language and thought. Not all. European scholars translated Sayana's narratives written in Sanskrit in the 1800's into bestsellers. But, sometimes incoherence and lack of connected thought in the translations lend themselves into mere prattle. When Sri Aurobindo along with Kapali Sastry in 1940's picked up the threads again, it was a new beginning to an ancient thought.

Sri Aurobindo expresses three terrifying deities under the trinity of Vishnu-Rudra-Brahmanaspati, which manifested as Vishnu-Shiva-Brahma in latter texts. Though, Rig Veda suggests no such trinity. Readers, please use your judgement and discretion on this.

Medhatithi Kanva

Agni, with your spouse, bring Soma loving Tvastar
Hotra's younger Bharati[54], and Varutri of the wise
Lodged in the vast, they protect from far
Their wings never clipped, women of paradise

1.22.9-1.22.11

Earth and heavens sprinkle the Yajna to its brink
Indrani, Varunani and Agnayi[55] join a Soma festive
Earth and heavens build Vipra a drink
Gandharvas agitated steps are active

1.22.12-1.22.14

Hey earth, pleasant is your flow of glory
Extensive is your sanctuary

1.22.15

May the gods, implant their power in us
And conclude the event set forth
Of Vishnu's strides
Across seven stations on earth

1.22.16

This Vishnu, he marched a beat
Thrice, he placed his foot
When in the dust of his feet
The new worlds were output

1.22.17

Guardian Vishnu, no contest
You paced the three splendid steps
Now you endorse the laws the best
From there flow the splendid effects

1.22.18

---

[54]Bharati and Varutri are spouses, younger sibling of the Hotra
[55]Every male principle has a counter female principle. Clearly shown here.

Behold Vishnu's endeavors
Flagrant are the laws of the universe
O friendly neighbors
Stay committed to Indra, not his converse

1.22.19

The wise only envision
They recall Vishnu's utmost stride
Extended are their sights, their mission
To the heavens, the images now guide

1.22.20

The chanting to inspire
Vigilant, enlightened prays the illumined seer
A knowledge so dear
Vishnu's splendid footstep, they hear

1.22.21

Dirghatama Auchathyah

Vishnu's colossal works, they approve
He sponsors every seat of accomplishment
Values the material worlds in his wide move
Just three steps are his universal movement

1.154.1

Vishnu sustains the high with his might
A dreadful bull in places of challenge
On the mountaintops lies his lair bright
Worlds domiciled. Three actions rearrange

1.154.2

Brisk turns our power of limbs and thought
Recall Vishnu, grazing highlands, far and wide
Singlehanded, he gauges a vast, lengthy cot
All this, with just three steady steps in stride

1.154.3

Three steps, replete with honey that perish not
Honeyed steps in ecstatic concord
Vishnu endorses the triple principle[56] untaught
Earth and heaven, he defends the other world

1.154.4

May I know why he made such a move?
When soul learns of god, why the arcane bliss?
Stationed high, Vishnu, the gods approve
Sweet congruence, a source of peace

1.154.5

Places, we seek at the end of life's journey
Where can we see many-horned herds of light?
Vishnu's wide-moving steps so worthy
In its manifold vastness, sparkling in white

1.154.6

His devout mind on the great hero is set
To Vishnu, a song of praise, a draught of juice
Moved by noble steeds, no gods run a threat
On the ridges of the hills Vishnu stands in recluse

1.155.1

A Soma drinker shrinks from a furious rush
Indra with Vishnu when they show their might
A mortal man silent at weapons that crush
They turn the bow armed Krisanu's arrow aside

1.155.2

Such offerings grow his manly fame
Parents, he brings to the genial flow therein
A son, he lowers, the father's premier name
The third set high in the light of heaven

1.155.3

---

[56]Triple principles of the three qualities - Satvik, Rajasik and Tamasik. Three
principles of creation, maintenance and annihilation

We laud his masculine power
Generous, guardian, safe with compassion
He marched, with three steps to the high tower
Crossed earth's realms for life, for freedom

1.155.4

A mortal man beholds his steps of two
Restless, he sees the light amazing
But his third step, none dare construe
Not even the birds who fly with their wing

1.155.5

He, a rounded wheel in a swift race
Sets ninety racing steeds with four
They see his vast form with songs of praise
A youth, he arrives on plea to our door

1.155.6

Far his shine, wide his fame, his grace
Like Mitra, help us while we feed you with oil
To Vishnu, the wise, this improved song of praise
Oblations paid in solemn rites as toil

1.156.1

He brings gifts to ancient Vishnu, the last
Vishnu adjudges, together with his spouse
He tells the story of Vishnu's high birth
He outshines in glory his peers in the house

1.156.2

Singers reckon if is he satisfied to the edge
Primeval germ of order is he right from birth
Recognizing him, have you told the sage?
Vishnu, may we enjoy your grace, no dearth

1.156.3

Royal Varuna and Ashvin twins await his will
The Marut host guides to enable
Vishnu's power seeks the day at still
With his friend he unbars the stable

1.156.4

Heavenly one takes a friendly nominee
Vishnu to Indra, godly to the godlier, their draw
The maker aids Arya from the world of three
Offers the worshipper his share of holy law

1.156.5

CONCLUSION

Vedas went through a crucial transitory period five to seven thousand years back when authors of spiritual and psychological texts snapped a new method to conceal the scriptures using cryptic material glyphs. Though these ancient texts never lost their true essence, the icons grabbed a dominant seat as they were easier to relate to the material world. People took advantage of the lost originals and introduced rituals and idol worship. Comprehended correctly, the scriptures suggest an aura which decrees not the profane, reveals their true substance to the initiated. The rituals stage a trap, which many stumble into when learning the Rig Veda. They miss the subtle Rig Veda promise of a deep appreciation of life and after-life.

The Rig Veda wisdom, the ancients thought was unfit, even dangerous to the ordinary human mind, in any case liable to misuse if revealed to vulgar, unpurified spirits. The cryptic grammar used in the ancient text remains undeciphered till date, many portions linger as mystery, but to the initiated mind, it is a clear imagery of man's evolution on earth moving to a destined refinement of transitioning to a higher creature.

Plato wrote in his notes that the essential form, the idea behind all things or the potency to create matter must have occurred in the primordial etheric space. The inner potency and the outer act complement this concealed idea to an outer form. Each acts as a symbol to the other.

The one immutable principle, which amounts to "nothing", is the creative aspect, but the cause of creation, a cause-less cause remains the true doctrine of every known scripture.

Divinity lies in the ineffable name of the nameless. Rig Veda promises the lost word that describes the nameless and the master-poets know its pronunciation and syntax. Each lord, fire, sun or system goes through a period of activity, followed by a period of repose. The creative process as understood from the Mantras of Agni and Vishnu never had a beginning and therefore no end. It is an endless succession of making-and-breaking. Just as the Sun, the many worlds materialize and disappear continually in a timescale we can only imagine. So do the mortals. But in a timescale that we can fathom.

Time has no future, nor any past. The authors of ancient scriptures recognized that the ear, a time organ could receive the etheric sound. They, however, did not associate the 'word' with 'time'. The word has no beginning or end. It is as prevalent today as it was, when they first conceived it.

In our terrestrially fertile minds, it is hard to conceive Lord Krishna's birth again, in a time that reoccurs in the past. When we understand the 'Kala' notion, the past, present and future become a blur. Then we comprehend that there was never a beginning, nor will there be an end. There was never a creation, nor can there be a destruction. Time stands still in a dimension we perceive not. The concept of the Supreme in the Rig Veda is a causeless cause or a rootless root. He never manifests before men. But, he pervades all. We cannot fathom or define it, but we know.

Justice rules the universe, the world. It is the symbol of permanency of a deity or the supreme god. It is the foundation of the Rig Vedic law. The symbolic law as in many chapters in Agni can mean the Karmic law that, as a creature sows, so shall he reap. No creature by the Rigvedic Law has any right to condemn and punish any other creature through his belief.

But, a veil of darkness hangs over us whose purport burnishes selfishness and hate. Under this dark canopy sleeps or wakes many a demon or sage, and one of them at any point in time breaks through the shackles. For no creature can serve two diverse masters.

Supreme Law is the permanency, quite the immutability of the divine being. Intelligence in nature is the divine order's harmony. Even Plotinus described, "God is not the principle of beings, but the principle of principles".

The etheric vacuity with room for every atom of matter and non-matter, is full of divinity. Described in Samudra Manthan, whose literal meaning is the churning of the ocean, the celestial ocean. When the world emanates and begins to manifest visibly, space becomes turgid. Like the curdling of milk. The invisible becomes visible. Turgid matter turns into dense matter. However, in the apparent chaos, order and formation continue unperturbed. In the churning, the invisible gems and poisons became apparent, the nectar of immortality, the permanency of the divinity becomes revealed. The churn in the far-out celestial region is the same churn within.

In the science of silence, practiced even today in the Monasteries in the Himalayas, when a person walks the rungs of ladder of self-knowledge, one pauses several times to stop, and listen to the inner voice at every seven rungs. At first, he hears a nightingale's (bulbul's) sweet voice singing a parting tunc. At the second rung, the sound of silver cymbals filter into his ears. Pausing at the third, the sound of the ocean spirit trapped in a conch shell greets him. Fourth, the melody of Veena plays softly. Fifth, comes the voice of a bamboo flute. At the sixth, he hears a trumpet blast. The last, seventh is a deep rumble of thunder clouds that drowns every other sound. With all six sounds frozen, the person merges at the ladder top as One with the supreme.

Scriptures often describe this journey through either seven, five or three stages. Vishnu's three majestic steps took him to the highest station, where he established the divine law. What Rig Vedic Vishnu achieved in three steps, other mortals and deities take seven or more. The texts associated the number seven with Agni. Later scriptures symbolized Agni as an icon possessing seven tongues of fire, surrounded by seven rays and auras of light. The texts often split the seven into four + three. In the septa-sonic advent, as the uninitiated reaches the higher rungs, he begins to 'hear the lights and see the sounds'. Color and sound are but a result of different vibrations. Matter exists on different planes, having different densities, different structure. Once you reverse or change the plane, you change the inherent or normal vibrations.

On each plane, or ladder rung, a dominant chord decides the 'notes' to which all vibrations conform. As in an octave of sounds, the plenary chords absorb the previous rungs of chords till there are no more.

Nature chooses matter to emerge as eternal arriving at the higher planes. The lower rung acts as the Upadhi-vehicle to assist in the higher climb. When laid to rest are all chords, and the incumbent merges with the One, the dual source of 'substance' and 'energy' become evident in the one ceaseless principle, often depicted as 'father-mother' in the texts as evident in the case of Agni. Consciousness stays incidental, appearing and disappearing from the physical plane. Though it is the permanent, basic factor of a creature's being, nothing destroys consciousness, except it tends to retire from one plane to another. Each creature is a miniature world evolving within the greater world. A wheel within a wheel. While there is the eternal knowledge and energy that is vast but unseen in the etheric space, there is a fragment of that intelligence in the small vacuity in the mind. When they are in harmony, the mortal in us turns into a vehicle for divine expression. The energies draw us closer to the deep bliss of the cosmic equilibrium, beyond the tenets of ritual lore to the inescapable reality we become one with the universe.

Expressed is Agni as inspiration, will, sacrifice, surrender and charity. The core of the Vedas is the controlled flame that is a sliver of untapped, divine energy. If we were to use this energy alone, there would be little need for anything more superficial? When Agni stays lit, the strength of the mind and senses whose lord is Indra and the invisible life force of Vayu come into play. Surya - the immense energy resource, the total of all energy is what we seek, what we long to go back to, and enjoin the forces in the steps of Vishnu. The Lapwing professes the Vedas as an instrument in seeing the eternal in everyday life.

COMMON SANSKRIT VERSES

a - to be
acha - pure
adhah - downward
adhvaram - sacrifice
ahah - daytime
aham - I
aksh - eye
ap - water - Apaha waters
api cha - or
aruhat - climb
asnute - enjoys, attains
astu - let it be
asva - horse
asya - of her, of this, faces
ava - down
barhih - of fire
bhava - of the divine
bhavan - yourself
bhesaja - medicine, healing power
ca - also, and, totally, thus, however
cana - looking upon
cano - sound
chet - intellect
cit - take care of, shine, observe
citra - wonderful
dadhi - yogurt
daiy (day) - to protect, to love
dha - support
dhenu - cow
dhi - buddhi, of the brain
disah - direction
dosa - bhuja, arms and shoulders - doh, dosah

durita - sin
dyo - heaven - dyam, dyvi
ehi - come near
eva - as well
ga - going, singing
gahi - chant
gira - speech
gl - moon
go - cow - gouh, gavey, gavi
havya - offering, oblation
hayah - horses
hita - agreeable, favor
hota - summon
hotra, hotri – priest
icch - desirous
idam - also, this (yah - this) - ayam, imam, asya, ime
imam - come this side
ime - all these
iva - like, as, as if, seemingly
jataveda - knowledge of all births and successions
jra - ageing - jarey, jaras
kim - who - kah, ken, kam, kasya
kva - where
ma - me
maha - shresta (first) not mighty
mama - mine
manas, manah - mind
manuswadagne – Manu's taste is fiery
mayi - unto me
mti - buddhi - murti
na - no
na cha - nor
nah - our
narasansa - praised by all men

ni - back, into, in, within, down
no - us
nou - boat - noah, nav
nr - human - na, narah, naram,
nu - certainly, at once
pari - around
pra - resemble
prasasta - bona fide
prati - about, to
prnita - created
punah - again
rajan - raja, king - rajne, ragyah
rishi - sage-poet-composer
rnaya - going after
rodasi - heavens, sky
rodasi - weep
rta - enlightened
ry - wealth - rma - laxmi; rah, ray; rasu
sa - that, with
sadan - seat
sanoh - peak
savitr - an Aditya, sometimes an attribute of Surya
sayutam – a bag
shruti - hear
shu - childbearing
soo - bring forth
srj – rush, hurled, let go
srudhi - listen
srva - complete - sarva, sarve - visva: complete
su - good, beautiful
sumat (along with or together)
syonakrit – one who spreads happiness
ta - they
tam - him

tana - one afer another
tanunapat - son of himself, self-made
tasang – stealthy, crawl like an animal
tat - that, third person he - sah, tau, ten, tebhya
te - they
tri - three - trye, trini, trishu
tu - and, but
tva - your, thy
tvam - you
tyad - third person - he
ubh - two
ubhe - ubh (cover)
uda - water
ukta - spoken
upa - near, more or less
upadhi - means
uta - or / or else
va - you
vaak - voice
vahata - carry
vaisvanara - one who treats all equally
vajavat – being strong.
vajinah - rich in horses
varenya - desirable
vari - water – as in vari, varini, varino
vastra - clothes
vasu - ray of light, beneficent, excellent
vayam - spoke
vedah - knowledge
vi - arrangement, order
vidmah - did know, do know
vish - subject – as in visah, vishay
visvan - dear to all men
visvaveda - omniscient, saint

vrishni - shower of knowledge
ya - travel
yahu - child
yaj – one who sacrifices, worshipping
yam - whom, which
yat - because, wherein, therefore
ye - those who, others, those persons
yena - wherefore, as, on which account
yo - who, that
yuj - assemble

THE DEITIES

Agni: Fire metaphor. A cosmic power of heat, light, power of will, and wisdom. Human will-power pales in front of this power. R.L. Kashyap writes 'Man can strengthen the power of will by Veda mantras of Agni.'

Indra: Symbolizes the Divine Mind and Action Lord. Indra battles the evil forces on behalf of the human.

Vayu: Wind Metaphor. He is the Lord of all the Life-energies, which represent the passions, feelings, emotions and abilities.

Ashvins: The twins are the Rulers of Bliss and Divine. They are the celestial physicians who free the human body of disease.

Mitra: The Lord of Love and Harmony.

Varuna: The Master of 'vastness' who tolerates not restrictions in thought and actions.

Sarasvati: The Goddess of inspiration.

Ila: The Goddess of revelation.

Surya: The Supreme Deity of Light and Force.

Aditi: The mother of the seven gods. She is the Goddess of the etheric space.

Bhaga: Enjoyer and the Distributor of Delight.

Brahmanaspati: Lord of Mantra, also sometimes referred as Ganapati.

Maruts: Twins and a team. Represent the Life Energies.

Rudra: The Force of Evolution.

Soma: The Divine Delight.

Vaisvanara: Universal Divine Will and Force.

Vasu: The master of riches.

Vishnu: The Lord of all Etheric Space.

Pushan: The deity of nourishment.

POPULAR GLYPHS

Common themes set as icons and glyphs come into view in Rig Veda throughout. Interspersed are the horse (steed), cow (cattle), son and hero in every Mantra. R.L. Kashyap writes that 'Sons or children are new soul-formations, which constitute the divine personality, symbolically - new births within us. Heroes are mental and moral energies which resist the assaults of ignorance, division, evil and falsehood.'

He further writes 'The vital powers motivate us on our journey and a horse symbolizes them. The herds of cows (sometimes cattle) are powerful illuminations that arrive from the supramental truth, or the herding rays of the light of the Sun.'

REFERENCES

Rig Veda Samhita Vols 1 through 10 – R. L. Kashyap, SAKSHI, Bengaluru, 2016 (in English and Sanskrit)

Rig Veda, Vols 1 through 10 – Dr. Ganga Sahay Sharma, Sanskrit Sahitya Prakashan, New Delhi (in Sanskrit)

Rigveda Samhita - Shrimatsayanacharya Virachit Bhasya sametha by Vaidic Samshodhana Mandala, Tilak Maharashtra University, 1933 (in Sanskrit)

The Rigveda. 1886. The oldest literature of the Indians – Adolf Kaegi, Zurich. Authorized Translations by R. Arrowsmith.

The Hymns of the Rigveda - Translated by Ralph T. H. Griffith 2nd edition, Kotagiri (Nilgiri) 1896

The Sacred Books of the East – F. Max Muller. Vol XXXII. Oxford, printed at the Clarendon Press. 1891.

Further Lights on the VEDA – T.V. Kapali Sastry, SAKSHI, Bengaluru.

The Indus Script and the Rg-veda, 1997 – Egbert Richter-Ushanas, Motilal Banarsidass Publications, Delhi

Call of the Vedas, Fourth Ed - A.C. Bose. Bhartiya Vidya Bhavan, Mumbai.

Rup-chandrika - Brahmananda Tripati by Choukhamba Surbharati Prakashan, Varanasi (in Sanskrit)

Essentials of Rig Veda - R.L. Kashyap. SAKSHI 2009

Secret of the Veda - Sri Aurobindo, Lotus Press 1995

Hymns to the Mystic Fire - Sri Aurobindo, Lotus Press 1996

Hymns of the Rig-Veda - Translation by Jean Le Mee, 1995 Bonzoi Book

Akhenaten, Surya, and the Rigveda – Subhash Kak, 2003

Satya Prakash Saraswat, Ph. D. Professor of Computer Information Systems. Bentley College. Waltham MA-02452.

Yajna - Physical and Subtle – R.L. Kashyap, SAKSHI, Bengaluru

Veda Knowledge in the Modern Context – R.L. Kashyap, SAKSHI, Bengaluru

Exploring the Mystery of the Gods (Ashvins, Usha, Rbhus, Maruts, Pushan, Soma, Varuna and Vishvedevah) – R.L. Kashyap, SAKSHI Bengaluru

Code Agni – Dev Bhattacharyya, Devb Inc, USA

AUTHOR

Dev Bhattacharyya like many other authors became indoctrinated into the art of writing. In this book, the author has chosen not to let style rule over content. Dev writes books on Vedas, articles on many journals in the past and a book on technology. Dev lives with his wife and children in the northeast United States and is a prolific reader.

www.ingramcontent.com/pod-product-compliance
Lightning Source LLC
LaVergne TN
LVHW011202080426
835508LV00007B/547